A Mirror of Our Dreams
Children and the Theatre in Canada

A Mirror of Our Dreams

Children and the Theatre in Canada

Joyce Doolittle & Zina Barnieh

with a chapter on Theatre in Québec
by Hélène Beauchamp

Vancouver, Talonbooks, 1979

copyright © 1979 Joyce Doolittle, Zina Barnieh and Hélène Beauchamp

published with assistance from the Canada Council and the University of Calgary, Calgary, Alberta.

Talonbooks
201 1019 East Cordova
Vancouver
British Columbia V6A 1M8
Canada

This book was typeset by Pulp Press, designed by David Robinson and printed by Hemlock Printers for Talonbooks.

Some of the material in this book has appeared in *Canadian Theatre Review (CTR 18)* as "Theatre for the Young: Happy Un-birthday Words" by Joyce Doolittle and in *Canadian Children's Literature, Number 8/9* as "Some Myths in Canadian Theatre for Young Audiences" by Zina Barnieh.

Talonplays are edited by Peter Hay.

First printing: April 1979

Canadian Cataloguing in Publication Data

Doolittle, Joyce, 1928-
        A mirror of our dreams

        Bibliography: p. 188
        Includes index.
        ISBN 0-88922-161-8 pa.

    1. Children's plays - Presentation, etc. - Canada. I. Barnieh, Zina, 1945-   II. Beauchamp, Hélène, 1943-   III. Title.
PN3157.D65   792'.0226'0971   C79-091133-7

This book is dedicated to
Sue Kramer

The deepest kind of recognition. . .occurs when we
say to ourselves of what is going on onstage: "I know
I have never seen that before but I know it is true."
It occurs when what we see onstage draws together
for us thoughts, aspirations and sympathies we have
not yet articulated for ourselves, or not yet combined. It occurs when the action onstage taps the
dark part of our imagination and becomes the
mirror of our dreams. This is what recognition in
the theatre aspires to be: *re-cognition* — thinking, or
imagining, again.

Jonathan Levy, Playwright
from an Address Delivered
at the University of Calgary,
February, 1972

Table of Contents

Preface

Some years ago, I was shocked to learn that about half of all professional activities in the Canadian theatre were directed at children and young audiences. The reprehensible part of this discovery was the realization that this half received only about five percent of the funding that goes to so-called adult theatre. In terms of less tangible support — esteem and qualified criticism — the imbalance is even greater. During almost ten years as a theatre critic, I have seldom reviewed a performance for children. And it took the same decade, until this Year of the Child, for Talonbooks to launch a series of scripts emerging from young people's theatres.

This book for me is not just one of expiation. It is one of remembrance. In Central Europe, I grew up with professional theatre from the earliest age. There was a puppet theatre and more than one company playing to children of different ages. All of them had a permanent building, played all year round and were subsidized on an equal footing with the other theatres that catered to grown-ups. And there are memories of the past decade here in Canada. The anger, as I watched how The Vancouver Playhouse courted and made a marriage of convenience with the older Holiday Theatre, selling off the building that Holiday paid as dowry, then degrading and finally destroying her. Good memories, too. During an interview with John Neville, hearing him tell what attracted him to take the job as artistic director of Citadel Theatre: a photograph of the troupe from Citadel-on-Wheels in the Arctic surrounded by Inuit children. And the warm days in the spring of 1978, in Vancouver's Vanier Park, during the first International Theatre Festival for Children: the excitement radiating from the tents, and performances so much more alive and immediate than what one normally experiences in the adult theatre.

So this is a special book appearing in a special year. It celebrates not only the children, but also the child in each one of us. The heroes of this book are magicians, who foster in hundreds of thousands of children the sense of wonder that all good theatre has in abundance.

And the people who wrote this book are also special. Joyce Doolittle. She has been international vice-president of ASSITEJ (the World Organization of Theatre for Children and Youth) since 1972, having founded the Canadian Centre in 1968 and directed it for its first decade. Apart from acting, directing and teaching fulltime at the University of Calgary, she has been tireless in developing theatre for young audiences in Canada. Similarly, Zina Barnieh has a varied background in teaching, acting, directing and involvement with ASSITEJ. She has been adapting and writing Lewis Carroll stories for production at the Pumphouse Theatre in Calgary, in which Joyce and her composer-husband, Quenten Doolittle, have been collaborating. No other two individuals could have given this perspective on theatre for young audiences in English Canada in terms of research, practical knowledge and personal involvement, and with such understanding and generosity. I am also grateful to Hélène Beauchamp for her valuable overview of French-language theatre for young audiences. She has both taught history of the theatre and produced new works by Québécois authors at the University of Ottawa, and she is an expert on contemporary French theatre in Canada.

Finally, I would like to thank the University of Calgary for its grant towards publication of this specialized book, without which its production by Talonbooks would not have been possible.

Peter Hay
Fort Langley, B.C.
April, 1979

10

Introduction

This book addresses itself to a specialized subject: professional theatre for young audiences in Canada. It is not about theatre by the young or by amateurs. Professional theatre for children in Canada began in 1953 when Joy Coghill and Myra Benson established the Holiday Theatre in Vancouver. That is no great age for a movement or art form, but, as with a person of twenty-six, certain observations about appearance, accomplishments and philosophy may be made and hopes for the future may be expressed.

We began working on the book in 1973. We had acted as hosts for five hundred delegates from all over the world to the Fourth General Assembly of ASSITEJ (the Association International du Théâtre pour l'Enfants et la Jeunesse) in Montréal. We realized there how little had been written and published about the growing phenomenon of theatre for young audiences. Research has taken both authors from North America, coast to coast, and to Europe more than twenty times. Everywhere we met people who were extraordinarily dedicated and committed to their work. But in Canada, given the vast distances and scant resources — especially during the gruelling school tours — the energy, concentration and endurance, demanded and given, are far beyond the common call of duty. We salute these modern-day mummers who move through the small towns and large cities of our country and speak to our children with many voices.

The history of theatre for young audiences in Canada has been discussed elsewhere: in an unpublished dissertation by Dr. Teresa MacKinnon, and in a leading article by Joyce Doolittle, co-author of this book, for the special issue of the *Canadian Theatre Review (CTR 10)* devoted to the subject. This book does not aim to duplicate those efforts.

What we have tried to do instead is to give an overview, and present the main challenges facing theatre for young audiences as we enter the 1980's. From the more than three dozen equity companies now in the field, we have selected for closer study some of the few whose stability is reflected in the continuity of artistic direction from inception to the present, and whose repertoire derives its main strength from the region in which they play. The companies chosen by these criteria are: Mermaid

Theatre of Wolfville, Nova Scotia; Globe Theatre of Regina, Saskatchewan; and Alberta Theatre Projects of Calgary. We also include a section on Young People's Theatre in Toronto, the first theatre to have a home of its own entirely dedicated to performances for young people.

We have been fortunate in obtaining a chapter about the explosion of theatre activities for young audiences in Québec. Hélène Beauchamp, the author, is an expert who has contributed criticism and chronicled extensively the field in Québec.

Although for the purposes of this book we equated "professional" with "equity", the word does and ought to mean more than contracts and money. The rewards of producing and performing for young people are enormous for those few whose heart and lifelong career are dedicated to this field. But they tend to be negligible and even negative for the many more who find themselves working for children because it is the first or only job in the professional theatre that they can get. We hope with this book to call attention to all of the theatre artists in Canada who have contributed to the generally rising standards we now enjoy in theatre for the young. The objectives of professional theatre for young audiences should be the same as for all art. In this book, we discuss these aesthetic aspirations and ideals so that even greater achievements may follow.

Joyce Doolittle
Zina Barnieh
Calgary, Alberta
April, 1979

Part One
Today's Child
and the Theatre

Changing Concepts of Childhood

The twentieth century can be justly proud of the care given to the problems of childhood. Pre-natal clinics, generally safe birth techniques, child development, safety and welfare have dramatically reduced early mortality. Child labour laws have all but abolished the exploitation of minors by business and industry. Universal and free public education provide opportunities for all young people. Prior to the late Renaissance, survival itself was the qualifier for adult life. This is still true for many in today's Third World countries; but among industrialized nations, it is an unfortunate exception, not the general rule.

With the creation of childhood as a separate and increasingly sheltered time of life, specialized services and goods began gradually to appear. Distinct clothing for children could be noted in the 17th century. Schools (for male children) became more widespread in the 18th century. Literature for children, begun in the same period, exploded during the next century. Theatre for children is an invention of our era — an infant art form. How does it affect today's child and where does it fit in with our idea of childhood?

There are widely held beliefs that childhood is for children only, that children should be protected, that childhood is a joyous and carefree period of life. But, with these, we turn childhood into a ghetto, no matter how attractively decorated with fairy tale figures and myths now stripped of their original power and truth. We also use them to deny children the power to make decisions in important aspects of their lives until a magic number of birthdays (sixteen, eighteen or twenty-one) has passed. There is an underlying feeling that, while childhood is a glorious place for children, one would not wish to return there: that small things for small persons are small in significance. This attitude pervades most adult assessment of theatre for young people. (Charming perhaps, but childish.) It is, in part, a manifestation of the adult denial of "the child within" each human being throughout life. And the implications of that denial are serious. At a U.S. symposium on "Children's Television and the Arts" critic Richard Lewis said that we must recognize that childhood never ends: it is a continuing human endeavour. We see on television the ability of human beings to destroy themselves, to extinguish childhood and, according to him, what we need is a passion for the survival of childhood. An even deeper pessimism is expressed in the plays of Edward Bond, notably *Saved*, in which a baby is stoned to death by youths. In a preface to his *Lear*, Bond writes about *kindermord*:

> I write about violence as naturally as Jane
> Austen wrote about manners. Violence shapes
> and obsesses our society, and if we do not stop
> being violent we have no future. [1]
>
> Every child is born with certain biological
> expectations, or if you like species' assumptions
> — that its unpreparedness will be cared for,
> that it will be given not only food but emotional
> reassurance, that its vulnerability will be
> shielded, that it will be born into a world
> wanting to receive it. But the weight of aggres-
> sion in our society is so heavy that the unthink-
> able happens: we batter it. And when the
> violence is not so crude it is still there, spread
> thinly over years; the final effect is the same
> and so the dramatic metaphor I used to des-
> cribe it was the stoning of a baby in its pram.
> This is not done by thugs but by people who
> like plays condemning thugs. [2]

Generally, our children are not so much stoned as suffocated. The torrent of trivia, at its best mere diversion and at its worst the cynical exploitation of an unsophisticated and open audience, must be matched with thoughtful and joyful offerings. One often hears the remark, "But the children loved it!" about a theatrical production for children whose professional standards were found wanting in some way. Unless an enthusiasm for the piece is evident in the accompanying adults, it does not deserve praise. The American drama critic Dan Sullivan has said that good children's theatre brings out the child in the man. As adults, we should enjoy the plays as much as children and recognize something of ourselves in their response. Contact with "the child within" is evident in many

16

authors and artists who create works also for young people. Dennis Lee, whose poems appeal to both children and adults, has said:

> And the key to writing for children, for me at least, is to get in touch with one of those children in myself and then follow his nose, going wherever the child's interest leads me — whether or not the adult in me is also pleased. Ideally, they both will be.
>
> And if the two do fuse with one another — the adult integrity, which has had the chance to *be* integrity because it has been tested so many times, been deflowered so often, and the child's capacity for play — if the two do fuse, in the writing and then in the reading, there can arise the kind of simplicity which occasionally comes into being on the other side of complexity. This matters. It means children's literature mediates something that is found in lyric poems and songs, and is more commonly noticed there by critics: that is, a distillation or unification of experience. [3]

We need both adult integrity and child's play in our offerings for children. That play is important to adults as well as to children must be more generally recognized and opportunities for it provided. Dennis Lee, again:

> I take play to be one of the primary estates of being human, as fundamental as eating, pro-creating, congregating, being conscious. The inhibition and the relative atrophy of that instinct in adulthood seems to me one of the disaster areas of our civilization. [4]

Another Canadian author who has paid attention to both play and the "child within" is James Reaney. In "Kids and Crossovers" written for the *Canadian Theatre Review (CTR 10)*, Reaney discusses the links between the workshops his actors conducted with boys and girls in the morning, and the creation of the adult Donnelly trilogy in the afternoons in Halifax in the summer of 1973. But his commitment to play, his seriousness about both children and the "child within," and the implications of these on theatrical creation, go back much further:

> Reaney in London became more and more in-
> terested in children's theatre. Such a theatre,
> he believed, should not and need not exclude
> adults. The staying power of nursery rhymes
> and fairy tales depends, he argues, upon the
> fact that adults enjoy reading them to children.
> Indeed, Reaney has suggested, children's clas-
> sics are far more sophisticated and demanding
> than most so-called adult literature which, by
> being adult, has lost its belief in metaphor. The
> children's theatre he had in mind, therefore,
> was a children's theatre for adults. The adult
> world of the twentieth century tends, according
> to Reaney, to take for granted C.P. Snow's no-
> tion of the two cultures, or like F.R. Leavis, im-
> poses in the classroom certain moral impera-
> tives upon literature which are alien to the ima-
> gination. Metaphor, for Reaney, is its own jus-
> tification, and those who affirm it for its own
> sake affirm the true identity-confirming activity
> of man. The child's world is metaphor and, as
> such, human and civilized. Each act of the ima-
> gination is a recovery of it, a restoration and a
> rebirth.[5]

Writers of children's literature believe that adults should enjoy works for children and that, ideally, such enjoyment will put them in touch again with the child within themselves. The collection of writings on children's literature, *Only Connect*, furnishes the following examples:

> The making of children's picture books is in-
> deed like playing with children. The game is on
> even when the author-illustrator sits alone at his

drawing table. For he is not really as lonely as he seems to be. He has his abstract public with him, as have artists in every field. In his case, it is a public made up of two kinds of children. First, there is the child he was, a child who is very much present and who inspires him and helps him understand the other children. Second, there are the abstract children who are watching over his shoulder.[6]

. . . .My own children's books. . . .were, of course, written and illustrated to amuse the children, and I hope the poor grown-ups who have to read them over and over again do not find them too irksome. But all the same, they were still written largely to amuse that childish part of myself. I am afraid this is an awful confession to make, but alas I am not only incorrigible but also unrepentant, and so will go on concocting new works merely for the fun of it.[7]

. . . .Not that I basically write for children. I really do these books for myself. It's something I have to do and it's the only thing I want to do. Reaching the kids is important, but secondary. First, always, I have to reach and keep hold of the child in me.[8]

Maurice Sendak and Dennis Lee have similar things to say about the reality and importance of their "child within." Sendak says:

You see, I don't believe, in a way, that the kid I was grew up into me. . . .He still exists somewhere, in the most graphic, plastic, physical way. It's as if he had moved somewhere. I have a tremendous concern for him and interest in him. I communicate with him — or try to — all the time. One of my worst fears is losing contact with him.[9]

Dennis Lee claims he has more than one child inside:

> Like most adults, I have a number of children
> trapped, held in suspension, in my nervous sys-
> tem. I can't find the right physical image for
> this, so I have trouble expressing the notion.
> But it is such an everyday experience that I
> don't question it.[10]

Fragmentation characterizes much of contemporary life and the separation of childhood and old age into specialized societies are two of the tragedies of our time. The impulses which led to the schism were humanitarian — albeit authoritarian. The old *should* be sheltered from poverty and neglect and the young *should* be protected against hunger, disease and exploitation. But our attitude toward childhood as a time of innocence is a relatively new one — and not without overtones of condescension:

> The idea of childish innocence resulted in two kinds of
> attitude and behaviour towards childhood: firstly, safe-
> guarding it against pollution by life, and particularly, the
> sexuality tolerated, if not approved of, among adults; and
> secondly, strengthening it by developing character and
> reason. We may see a contradiction here, for on the one
> hand childhood is preserved and on the other hand it is
> made older than its years; but the contradiction exists
> only for us of the twentieth century. The association of
> childhood with primitivism and irrationalism or prelogic-
> ism characterizes our contemporary concept of childhood.
> This concept made its appearance in Rousseau, but it
> belongs to twentieth century history.[11]

Perhaps it is this connection of childhood with primitivism and irrationality which leads to devaluation of works for children, of artists who create them and of the men and women who teach the young. Childhood and children are sentimentalized, but genuine respect for the real child or for that part of the adult which retains the imagination and joy of childhood is rarely encountered. A movement for the needs and rights of children has begun recently in the United States and now has a sizeable literature. One of the most prolific and convincing spokesmen of the rights of children is John Holt, whose book *Escape from Childhood* has popularized the same concerns quoted earlier from Edward Bond:

> People who feel they understand children and
> want to defend them often speak about them in
> a way that I used to agree with, but now find
> more and more often confused, sentimental, or
> misleading. They tell us that a child needs
> "time to grow" or that he should live in a "child's
> world" so that he may experience himself as "a
> human being in his own right." They speak of
> people trying to "destroy childhood" or "take
> childhood away from children."
>
> What is wrong with such words and ideas is
> that much of what they imply about children
> and childhood is not true, and what is true
> applies just as much to adults as to children.
> To whatever extent children really need what
> these words say they need, so do the rest of us
> young or old. To whatever extent we adults
> are denied those needs by the society and
> culture in which we live, so must children be
> denied them. When we say of children's needs,
> as of their virtues, that they belong only to
> children, we make them seem trivial, we invali-
> date them. What is more important, we insure
> that they will not be met. For no amount of
> sentimentalizing or preaching will make a
> society provide for its young people a better
> quality of life than it provides for its adults.
> We fool ourselves if we think ways can be found
> to give children what all the rest of us so sorely
> lack.[12]

Until childhood has a different and better status in our society, how can one expect theatre for young audiences to have a different or better status?

Our democratic idea of independence, popularized and

idolized in the slogan "do your own thing," has not led to uplifting and enlightenment in our society. Instead, many would claim that it has led to a bland homogeneity in which the opportunity to exercise individuality consists, in large part, in the freedom to choose your own brand of toothpaste or deodorant. Ample documentation now exists that today's children sing television commercials as naturally as former generations chanted nursery rhymes and playground games. Television may enable today's North American child to know more about the world, but it also means that he knows more about consumerism — on both a conscious and unconscious level. The cynicism developed as a protection against the hucksterism of commercials has been a potent factor in eroding the remaining innocence of childhood in the past generation.

The fight to obtain what Richard Farson has called "birthrights" for children has had little impact upon the literature or arts offered to our young people. Farson lists in his child's bill of rights the following:

> The right to a single standard for adults and children. (Children should not have a special set of morals and rules for behaviour.)

> The right to alternative home environments. (Today, children must live with their parents or be placed in reformatories.)

> The right to responsive environmental design. (The entire man-made world has been designed for people who are at least five feet tall.)

> The right to education. (Freedom from school systems that systematically sacrifice individuality for uniformity, program children toward goals established by others and prohibit self-directed learning.)

> The right to freedom from physical punishment. (Adults simply should not be allowed to beat children.)

The right to sexual freedom.
(Early access to birth control information and
devices; liberation from sex-role stereotyping.)

The right to economic power.
(Freedom to work at any job as an alternative
to compulsory education.)

The right to political power.
(Child citizens are now denied the vote —
although suffrage is granted to the senile, the
mentally defective, the schizophrenic and the
alcoholic.)

The right to justice.
(Reform of the juvenile justice system which is
more unfair, arbitrary, cruel and repressive
than the corresponding adult criminal justice
system.)[13]

Is society ready to reconsider the institution of childhood
and give children these "birthrights?" It seems unlikely. The
decline in the birthrate in many countries has improved the lot
of children, but two extreme poles of parental behaviour have
surfaced more and more publicly — child abuse and "the child
as pet." In Canada, one outstanding example in the arts of
attention being paid to the rights of children is Mordecai
Richler's book, *Jacob Two-Two Meets the Hooded Fang*. The
trial of Jacob Two-Two is a model of adult injustice to
children; the denouement in which the Hooded Fang is found
to have "a child inside" illustrates the degree to which our
society punishes both the child and the very attributes (in
adults) which we claim to value most in children. The Richler
book has been made into a film and at least two staged versions
appeared in 1979.[14] More such incisive satire would be
welcome in our theatre repertoire for children.

In our age of accountability, the need to justify expenditures
on the arts grows. For theatre in general and theatre for young
people in particular, a belief in the unbelievable — fantasy,
imagination, myth and metaphor — is the most potent
argument we have. No one will deny that the body and even

the mind need food. But food for the spirit is suspect. It is our belief that such nourishment is equally essential; indeed, that it is impossible for a human being to be complete and whole without attention to all three facets throughout life. It is time to re-evaluate and enlarge our concept of childhood, to value the child within the adult, and to nurture the qualities of the child, such as innocence and imagination, so widely praised but poorly served in our society. The arts are essential to this process and theatre provides powerful and unique tools for this critical work.

Footnotes

1. Bond, Edward. "Author's Preface," *Lear*, Methuen, London, 1972, p.v.
2. *Ibid.*, p. viii.
3. Lee, Dennis. "Roots and Play: Writing as a 35 Year Old Children." *Children's Literature Quarterly*, No. 4, p. 35.
4. *Ibid.*, p. 45.
5. Woodman, Ross. *James Reaney*, Canadian Writers #12, New Canadian Library Original, McClelland and Stewart Limited, Toronto/ Montreal, 1971, p. 27.
6. Duvoisin, Roger. "Children's Book Illustration," Reprinted in *Only Connect*, Edited by Sheila Egoff, G.T. Stubbs and L.E. Ashley, Oxford University Press, Toronto, 1969, p. 358.
7. Ardizzone, Edward. "Creation of a Picture Book," *op. cit.*, Egoff, Stubbs and Ashley, p. 356.
8. Hentoff, Nat. "Among Wild Things,"*op. cit.*, Egoff, Stubbs and Ashley, p. 346.
9. *Ibid.*, p. 329
10. Lee, Dennis, *op. cit.*, p. 30.
11. Ariès, Philippe. *Centuries of Childhood*, Translated from the French by Robert Baldick, Vintage Books, New York, 1962, p. 119.
12. Holt, John. *Escape from Childhood*, Ballantine Books, New York, 1974, p. 105.
13. Farson, Richard. *Birthrights, A Bill of Rights for Children*, Macmillan, New York, 1974.
14. In Calgary, Storybook Theatre produced *Jacob Two-Two* in its amateur theatre season as an improvised piece. In Toronto, Young People's Theatre presented the Richler classic, as adapted by Pat Patterson, Dodi Robb, Joy Alexander and Peg McKelvey. The YPT version directed by Stephen Katz will represent Canada at the Young Vic in London, England in October, 1979.

Arts and Children in Canada

Most Canadian children do not suffer from malnutrition and almost all have the opportunity for education. There are the obvious problems of child abuse, drug addiction and children's rights and the more subtle concern with the *quality* of Canadian life, which provides for physical and social comforts, but often neglects the spirit and the soul. Canadian children have leisure time and most have access to various cultural resources. But what is the *quality* of these offerings for our young people? Although quantity is still a concern in some small centres and in remote areas, it is to this question of quality we would like to address ourselves. It is not enough to be thankful for a comfortable life, we must also consider whether physical comforts may not be hiding culturally and emotionally arid citizens. Sir Herbert Read has eloquently voiced this concern:

> . . . .Cultivation of the arts is an education of
> the sensibilities, and if we are not given an edu-
> cation of this kind, if our hands remain empty
> and our perception of form is unexercised, then
> in idleness and vacancy we revert to violence
> and crime.[1]

Is Canada providing an "education of the sensibilities" for its young? The answer need not lie in the establishment of yet another course or curriculum in "cultural education," rather in examining what our children are offered by the normal environment.

A picture of Canadian cultural life is not altogether depressing. In the past twenty-five years theatre for young audiences — as one example of a cultural resource available to the young — has developed considerably. It is beginning to achieve an acceptable, and in some cases, excellent artistic standard. One can be cautiously optimistic about future growth toward further excellence. The director of the Canada Council, Charles Lussier, has stated:

> It is of immense importance to the world that a
> country that used to be at the edge of the earth

and is now a kind of global Switzerland surrounded by all the world's great powers should
have achieved the repatriating of its culture.
For this is essentially what has happened in the
last twenty years, in all parts of Canada, and
what was once an inarticulate space on a map
is now responding to the world with the tongues
and eyes of a disciplined imagination.[2]

Today, Canada has a larger number of companies performing
Canadian material, often of a high artistic quality, than ever
before. Where does theatre for young audiences go from here?
What place should it have in the lives of Canadian children?
How many children experience live theatre? Growth does not
mean that all children have equal opportunities. Many young
people may see only one play a year, usually the school production. And how it affects them would be impossible to answer.
Most parents have little or no voice in deciding about theatre in
the schools. Few of them seek out weekend performances of
plays for their children. But even in these cases, one suspects
children are being taken to the theatre for entertainment and
cultural training and not for reasons of personal awareness or
genuine enlightenment about one's place in life. Perhaps this
last reason will be judged as pretentious or platitudinous, but
performance should never offer less than discovery about the
viewer's identity in the world. Adults, transmitting values to
their young, affect the role that art plays in life. Canadian
citizens accept, without question, certain kinds of time-
consuming, unnourishing entertainment without demanding
change in popular programming. Many televison, movie and
theatre experiences are very superficial. The acceptance of
superficiality in an activity which should be a deep one
infiltrates all other aspects of living:

We use the senses to arouse passion, but not to
fulfill the interest of insight, not because that
interest is not potentially present in the exercise
of sense, but because we yield to conditions of
living that force sense to be an excitation on the
surface.[3]

Our costly and omnipresent media hypnotizers are seldom employed in nobler purposes. North American television in particular transmits for the longest number of hours the poorest overall quality of programming in the world.

The arts, including theatre for young audiences, can heighten life. Works of art give crystallized focus on life. Some identification happens on a conscious level—sensing, feeling, verbalizing—and some in the unconscious: images, sounds, rhythms. We can no more escape the dominant rhythms, sounds and images of our own times than we can stop breathing. We need to have these composed with genius and compassion in our contemporary art forms. One of the main benefits of live theatre is that it offers an opportunity for a greater and deeper range of experience than would be possible in any one person's life. It affords a vicarious opportunity to play what Stanislavski called the "magic if" game. The power of live theatre comes, in large measure, from the audience. The audience is *necessary* to the event, the players are real and touchable, although the play they perform may transcend everyday reality.

The role of art in society is not only for cultural awareness but also for cultural transfer. Dewey comments:

Aesthetic experience is a manifestation, a
record and celebration of the life of a
civilization, a means of promoting its development, and is also the ultimate judgement upon
the quality of a civilization.[4]

Some theatres for young audiences believe their role to be social catalysts to make their audiences actively aware of the needs for change. For some, therefore, theatre is an agit-prop tool to provoke social change.

Specialized art forms for the young are a recent phenomenon in literature, theatre, film and television. The visual arts and music have few pieces created specially for children. Some people question whether there should be any works of art designated for children. Many would agree that a satisfying work for children must also satisfy an adult audience. W.H. Auden is emphatic on this point in his essay on Lewis Carroll's *Alice* books:

There are good books which are only for adults, because their comprehension presupposes adult experiences, but there are no good books which are only for children. A child who enjoys *Alice in Wonderland* and *Through the Looking Glass*) will continue to enjoy them when he or she is grown up, though his "reading" of what they mean will probably change.[5]

In some cases, specialization of the professional arts for the young has meant a loss in quality. A work of art that is specifically prepared for a young audience must have the same aesthetic criteria as art for any age group. There must be enough substance in a play for children to hold also an adult audience or its validity must be questioned. For producers, parents and teachers who care about the quality of experiences for young people, the following list of questions, asked by Edward Rosenheim, Jr. about children's books may be applied to playscripts and performance as well:

Will this book call into play my child's imagination? Will it invite the exercise of compassion or humour or even irony? Will it exploit his capacity for being curious? Will its language challenge his awareness of rhythms and structures? Will its characters call for — and even strengthen — his understanding of human motives and circumstances, of causes and effects? and will it provide him with a joy that is in some part the joy of achievement, of understanding, of triumphant encounter with the new?[6]

Footnotes

1. Read, Sir Herbert. "Art and Life: Adventures of the Mind 36," *The Saturday Evening Post,* CCXXXII, September 26, 1959, p. 106.
2. Lussier, Charles. "The Canada Council: The Principle of Excellence and Its Implications in a Democratic Society," Notes for an Address, Harvard University, July, 1977, p. 9.
3. Dewey, John. *Art as Experience,* Minton, Balch and Co., New York, 1934. p. 21.
4. Dewey, John, *ibid.,* p. 326.
5. Phillips, Robert, ed. *Aspects of Alice: Lewis Carroll's Dream-child as Seen through the Critics' Looking Glasses.* Vanguard, New York, 1971, p. 20.
6. Rosenheim, Edward W. "Children's Reading and Adults' Values," *op cit.* Egoff, Stubbs and Ashley, p. 20.

Live Theatre

In the short life span of Theatre for Young Audiences in Canada, several myths have evolved. Some people live by them and make choices accordingly. These reflect cultural attitudes in both professional and lay members of the theatre community. Many of the most tenaciously held myths are connected with adult perceptions of the child audience.

Myth One: Children are the most difficult audience to please.

Every theatre company has proof of its ability to please a child audience. Collections of drawings, photographs and letters fill file drawers across Canada. Observers watching child audiences take delight in pointing to the intense absorption of children watching a play. Judging pleasure and satisfaction is more complicated. One could interview members of the same audience after a show and gather reactions on a continuum of opinion from "terrible" to "terrific," with "I don't know" and timid giggles in between.

How does one determine pleasurable or positive response to a production? Audiences, both young and adult, are generally inarticulate, cautious and unclear about their reaction to a play. Few have the candour or the opportunity for direct communication with the creators of the piece, as is shown in the following conversation in which a small boy approached Stuart Sherman after a performance of his *Third Spectacle*:

Boy:	I didn't get whether it was a magic show or not. What is it?
Sherman:	I like people to decide for themselves what it is. I have my ideas and you have yours.
Boy:	But what do *you* think it is?
Sherman:	Your ideas are as good as mine.
Boy:	I don't have any ideas.
Sherman:	Did you like it?
Boy:	I liked it, yeah.
Sherman:	But you're not sure what it was?
Boy:	No.

Sherman:	It doesn't matter really, as long as you liked it.
Boy:	What do *you* think it is? You said you had your own ideas.
Sherman:	My ideas? People think they're more important than they really are, just because I made up the show. I don't think my ideas are all that important.
Boy:	So you don't know what it really is? Your sign says *Third Spectacle*. What's your definition of *Third Spectacle*?
Sherman:	I did two before this one.
Boy:	Oh.[1]

Young people generally go to the theatre without expectations or demands. Values, appreciation and honest response to the theatre are learned by children from adults just as complacency or uncritical acceptance is imitated. The younger the child, the less able he is to verbalize his feelings, opinions and preferences. Analyzing pleasure, absorption and comprehension can easily become a subjective process rather than an objective description. Often, too, a child will say what he thinks the adult interviewer expects to hear. Ruth Frost, a child psychologist, has suggested that direct communication with children is perhaps the most useful way of researching response — provided the interviewer understands young people:

> If you want to know something about children
> ask them. This kind of interview is productive
> in direct proportion to going about it the right
> way. A frontal question like "What did you
> think about Peter Pan?" produces the reply,
> "It was good/bad" or simply a baffled look.
> Open-ended questions of the kind, "If you were
> boss of this whole play what would you do/or
> have changed?" may do to start. "When the
> boy had to choose, did he do the best thing?",
> "What do you think she meant when she said. .
> . . .?" "What do you think it was all about?"

Possibly some forced choices may be necessary, as
self-examination in children is not a natural
activity. Comments or observations of actions
are natural and interpretations are made
available if the interviewer sets the tone and
talks about specifics and not abstractions.[2]

Zinovy Korogodsky, artistic director of the Leningrad
Theatre of the Young Spectator, has said that when he first
began to work in theatre for the young he believed the myth
that children were the most difficult audience. Now he says he
believes the opposite. Children in their innocent and open
attitude toward all life experience, can be most easily duped
and ravished by the accoutrements of the theatre. The first
twenty minutes of any presentation will hold a young audience
merely through being a strong and immediate experience in a
strange surrounding — with the sights and sounds of the theatre
locale as much of a sensual experience for the young person as
the actual piece being presented. Children can be held by the
trivial, made to laugh at the obvious and brought back to
attention by a direct question from the stage. They are
susceptible to cheap theatrical tricks. One must become more
sensitive in judging the *quality* of the reactions before making a
judgement about how a particular piece has been received.
Jonathan Levy, a playwright whose work includes many pieces
for child audiences, once described different kinds of laughter
in the theatre:

Anyone who spends much time in
theatres — particularly in the backs of theatres
— learns to distinguish different kinds of
laughter. I don't mean just loud laughter and soft
laughter. I mean different *qualities* of laughter.

Some laughter is light, joyful and spontaneous.
It sounds like singing. It is laughter we are glad
to give. Other laughter is heavy and depressing. It sounds like barking, and we give it
grudgingly. Even as we laugh, we hate ourselves
for laughing and hate everyone concerned with
the play for *forcing us* to laugh.

> Go to the back of the house during a comedy
> for children. Listen to the *quality* of the
> laughter. So often the laughter is forced and
> mirthless. The children understand that they
> have been signalled to laugh — by the rhythm of
> the preceding line, by a big "take" or gesture,
> or some such trick — and they proceed to laugh
> because it is expected of them. But the laughter
> is of poor quality. It sounds canned. Often, it
> has an admixture of embarrassment in it.
>
> What disturbs me is that the humour of so
> many children's plays is *aiming* at this kind of
> laughter. Not trying for better and missing;
> aiming at it.[3]

The myth that children are a difficult audience allows producers of trivial plays with cheap humour to believe that "the children loved it." It would be better for all to agree with Korogodsky that children are the *easiest* audience and take gravely our responsibility to their innocent enthusiasm.

Myth Two: One can tell immediately if children don't like a play.

This myth is really a variation of the first myth of the difficult audience. The sight and sound of a child audience whose attention is *not* being held by a play is so terrifying to adults on both sides of the footlights, that it has given rise to the "most difficult" myth. It is true that a child audience, when obstreperous, is noisier and more physically rude than a bored audience of adults. The adult audience often falls asleep; the child audience frequently falls apart. But barring numbingly boring plays or patently unprofessional performances which lead to chaos in the audience, it becomes extremely difficult to judge whether children like or dislike a play. One may ask them, as Ruth Frost has advised. However, even an enlightened interviewer will find that recording answers will not necessarily illuminate the response. Interpretation goes beyond listening to words since children lack verbal agility:

Conversing with children is a unique art with
rules and meanings of its own. Children are
rarely naive in their communication. Their
messages are often in code that requires
deciphering.[4]

The art of deciphering is the key challenge to com-
prehending audience response. The reduction of this
challenge to simplistic generalized judgements about how
much "squirming" was "seen" is an oversimplification. This is
one challenge we hope scholars will accept in order to refine
the process of child audience evaluation.

Myth Three: We are preparing the audience of tomorrow.

To suggest that children go to the theatre as to a training
ground for the audiences that the adult regional theatres in
Canada crave is to degrade the whole field. Programs in
physical education are not undertaken to increase the number
of football, baseball or hockey fans, but for the intrinsic value
that skill and sportsmanship have for each individual child.
While it is true that exposure to any endeavour in childhood
may increase the chance that the activity will continue to
engage the interest of the individual as he matures, this cannot
be the *raison d'etre* for the activity. Children should be taught
to meet life head on—NOW—and theatre is uniquely
equipped to provide life experiences which are both powerful
and non-threatening. It is for the experience NOW that
theatre for young audiences should be played; any other
objective is cynical and unworthy of the name "live theatre." A
child, like any other person, should be encountered as a
dignified individual and not viewed as a future subscriber.

We need to rediscover the meaning of childhood and meet
the child in ourselves. Until we do this we will continue the
trivialization, exploitation and disrespect for the experience of
childhood that these "myths" illustrate.

Footnotes

1. McNamara, Brooks. "Stuart Sherman's Third Spectacle," *The Drama Review 70,* June, 1972, p. 47.
2. Frost, Ruth. "Notes on the Young Traveller," *Canadian Theatre Review (CTR 10),* Spring, 1976, p. 25.
3. Levy, Jonathan. "Modern Plays in Period Styles—The Uses of Tradition in Children's Theatre," An Address Given at the University of Calgary Open Lecture, February, 1972, pp. 16-17.
4. Ginott, Haim G. *Between Parent and Child,* Avon Books, New York, 1975, p. 21.

Television

> Imagine a science fiction movie like this: all
> across America children are playing happily.
> They read books, make up games together,
> explore the outdoors, and always mind their
> parents and teachers. Then one day mysterious
> boxes appear. In just a decade these boxes in-
> filtrate every American home and turn the
> children into zombies who cease to play
> outdoors, no longer want to read, and spend
> more time staring at the boxes than paying
> attention to parents and teachers. . . .[1]

So much has been discussed about children and television, and yet so little has been concluded. Only the impact of the medium is unarguable:

> Today over ninety-five percent of American
> households in all sectors of the country and of
> all income levels own at least one television set
> . . . .Pre-school children up to the age of six are
> the single heaviest television viewing audience
> in the United States.[2]

How does television affect young people in growing up, how does it work as a socializing force, and lastly, how does it help to shape the values and expectations in society?

Some argue that the types of characters children watch on television are the same as the archetypes given them in fairy tales. However, one must realize that while types may be vaguely similar, the process is different for the child. In viewing the visually explicit representations of conflict on television, the child is provided with elaborate and exact visual detail as well as embodied dialogue. In hearing or reading a fairy tale, the child is forced to fill in the visual and auditory details. Many believe that this mental imagery or "filling in" offers more opportunity for active identification and the working through of the child's own conflicts. With books, as in the oral tradition, the child has a better opportunity to identify with the archetypes offered whereas on television the child

37

views the event merely as "fact." Television viewing is a unique experience and cannot be compared to any other kind of experience (except to its close sister, the film) and we have yet to know the effect of the total process on the child.

One concern for many parents and teachers is the addictive nature of the medium. The *Detroit Free Press* conducted an experiment which involved the co-operation of five families for one month. The first surprise came with difficulties in finding couples willing to give up watching television completely for one month, even though the newspaper was offering a cash incentive of five hundred dollars. One hundred twenty households were contacted; ninety-three families turned down the proposal. Five families eventually participated. In a news account of the experiment it is reported that:

> The Callways, television "junkies" who logged
> seventy hours a week: both became nervous.
> His smoking jumped from a pack to two-and-a-
> half packs of cigarettes a day, while she suffered
> nervous headaches. . . .
>
> I was really surprised that there really did seem
> to be an addiction to television, with serious
> withdrawal symptoms. Some of these people
> almost literally went crazy. They didn't know
> how to cope.[3]

Television also becomes a background to most daily activities: playing, eating and even sleeping. The subliminal effect can be enormous. Television is a relatively passive activity. Over-indulgence is usually at the expense of spontaneity, conversation, curiosity, creativity, social life, responsibility, sensory exploration and reading. From television drama, children learn that conflicts are resolved quickly and easily, that force prevails and that there is "magic" in consumerism. The subtleties of life are rarely explored, the real struggles minimized, and the good always win — often with force. These values are not transmitted to all young people, and if and when they are, it is not the fault of television only. But many people do see a relationship between a boisterous and mentally passive child who watches a great deal of television and a sociable, attentive child who watches less. The big danger in a concentrated diet of television is that the viewer is not asked to reach out, to extend himself, or to become involved.

Educational television is a specific development for the young typified by the phenomenally successful American show, *Sesame Street*. Educational television uses the medium primarily for teaching concepts. The positive contribution is that it can offer the best teaching to the greatest number of students. The drawback of the electronic medium is its insensitivity to the viewer: there is no provision for feedback. The younger the person, the greater the need for two-way learning, if we wish to raise our children as spontaneous, flexible people. If we want predictable, imitative and unoriginal responses, then television is a helpful and efficient teacher.

Sesame Street is the world's most successful educational television program. Children as young as two years old recite the alphabet and count, much to the joy of parents whose toddler will ask to see "a-too-tweet." Business is booming with the millions of reproductions of Muppets, dolls, radios, sheets, toothbrushes, etc. One thing is crystal clear: infants, toddlers and children are vessels to be filled by whatever catches their attention. The question is, does *Sesame Street* light any fire in the child? Does it kindle imagination, curiosity and active involvement in the world?

The producers and professional artists associated with *Sesame Street* use the natural addiction of children to television and its unique potential to teach language skills, mathematical concepts, reasoning and problem-solving. It is an expensive show with the highest professional standards:

It is by any standard the largest educational
experiment ever. Children's Television
Workshop (CTW), which runs it, estimates on
the basis of Neilsen surveys that eight million
children see the show every week; and there are
probably six million who see three or more
shows every week. Though the cost works out to
only about one cent per exposure per child, the

total budget for the show runs to nearly
$8 million a year.[4]

The positive aspects of the medium are exploited to the
fullest:

> Television contains none of the emotional over-
> tones. A child may watch and learn by correct-
> ing his mistakes without fear of public exposure
> that occurs in classrooms. . . . Television's im-
> personality removes the constant threat of
> humiliation.

> We may regret the conditions in our society
> that make sanctuaries necessary and must
> guard against a child's permanent retreat into
> them, but sanctuaries are needed, and televi-
> sion is one of the few shelters children have.[5]

Test after test has proved the success of *Sesame Street's*
objectives. They have been achieved through great respect for
the child audience, carefully composed music and sound
effects, unexpected surprises, magical animation, action in
many forms and styles, a wonderful sense of humour and a
great variety in program segments. An adult can enjoy many
aspects of *Sesame Street*, since it is not "cute" or cloying. This,
too, was a part of the plan for the program:

> Running gags and blackouts, in the *Laugh-in*
> tradition, enchant adolescents and adults,
> which helps keep the set tuned to the channel
> on which *Sesame Street* appears. The youngest in
> the family, after all — this is another thing
> thought of ahead of time — doesn't control the
> set.[6]

On the other hand, some of the strengths are also,
potentially, the greatest weaknesses in this program. *Sesame
Street* is also responsible for:

> "Assaulting" their senses with its "frenetic

pace" and "psyched-up music". . . ."rote memorization" and putting a noose around children's ability to ever engage in sustained and developed thought.[7]

One could argue for or against the above, and of course it all depends on how much television is watched, what other activities the child is involved in, and whether or not other people interact with him and in what manner. The producers would agree that *Sesame Street* is only a part of a child's education, one which does not replace and cannot be replaced by other educational opportunities.

What about Canadian television for children? In the past, it does not appear to have had a high profile, apart from nostalgic stories of *Howdy Doody*. The CBC has been creating short Canadian segments used on *Sesame Street*. They appear to meet the high standard set by the show, offering profiles of Indian life and lessons in elementary French. CBC would like to produce longer segments and specials for network prime time, if it had the money, says John Kennedy, former head of children's programming. It does not seem to have high priority. Betty Lambert wrote candidly of her being commissioned a script for CBC television:

> So, what am I saying? I'm saying that when the
> CBC told me that all they wanted out of me was
> plot and "likeable" characters for *The Magic
> Lie*, they were insulting children, they were
> insulting me and they were ripping off the
> taxpayer, not to mention W.O. Mitchell. . . .
> Is it all right to put on crud when it's crud for
> children?. . . .Forgive me for writing that
> script. I wrote it, I finished it. I tried to stay
> true to the author's intention. But all the time
> I was certain of one thing. . . .children recog-
> nize the banal. Children recognize the cheap.[8]

Lambert says an admittedly second-rate U.S. science fiction story was chosen for adaptation for *The Magic Lie* series because "the CBC can't afford brilliant writers."

One famous Canadian, Marshall McLuhan, has voiced his

concern about the effects of television and accuses it of preventing viewers from taking an "inner trip," of:

> . . . . The loss of individual and personal mean-
> ing. . . . for violence, whether spiritual or
> physical, is a quest for identity and the
> meaningful. The less identity, the more
> violence.[9]

McLuhan suspects television is responsible for increasing symptoms of dyslexia: reading, writing and spelling disabilities combined with personality conflicts. He claims that where television is not available, dyslexia is not common.

Research about the effects of television violence on children has been extensive. Some of it claims violence as cathartic or morally supporting good against evil. Others warn of the dangers of role models, that violence is placed in too realistic a setting, that the viewer is desensitized, and thereby his or her aggression may increase.

Censoring violence adds another dilemma. Who is to define violence and therefore shape our values? Where does freedom of expression end and responsibility begin? If censoring violence is desirable, do we eliminate documentaries about war or prohibit *Roots*? More positively, if programming provided a wider social purpose and better entertainment, cops-and-robbers potboilers might drop in ratings and disappear.

The last biennial International Children's Television Conference judged North American children's television to be poor. Europeans called *Kidstuff*, a Canadian program with four child stars who look as if they are auditioning for the *Donny and Marie Show*, ". . . .plastic, spastic, and commercial."

> European technology is far superior to our own;
> they're able to achieve much sharper, clearer
> and more brilliant images. But the pace is
> slower, more leisurely, perhaps because there
> are fewer competing programs and viewers
> can't indulge in channel-hopping. (They find
> our shows too fast and frequently lacking in
> social purpose and controversy.)

Still, despite the Scandinavian insistence on moral significance, one of their most stunning productions was a simple outdoor adventure series, pure entertainment. . . . *The White Stone*, which won the Prix Jeunesse in 1974. The colour photography is breathtakingly beautiful and the acting by children is unlike anything we're used to: totally naturalistic and touching.

The winner this year? Again, it was a program that won because it was beautiful, poignant, and spoke to everyone. It combined art, skill and insight in a manner beyond the wildest hopes of its producers. It was called *Blind* and concerned two young friends, one sighted and the other blind, who shared each other's worlds for a day.[10]

Perhaps these types of programs could replace, at least in part, the many animated cartoons offered after school and on weekend mornings.

Ruth Frost has suggested that television dulls the appetite of young audiences:

Relations with humans at their best have periods of disappointment and when the child's experience is that people are too busy and always changing personnel he tends to become more interested in vivid and changing sensations, increasing novelty in the variety of experience and things happening very fast. Children's entertainment on television, until recently, has concentrated on pleasing through these techniques, short, simple and very striking presentations which change rapidly and involve a maximum of action, violence, humour and tension or suspense. These elements of how children have been trained prior to their first experience of live theatre must be taken into consideration. A pattern of expectation has already been set. If commercial interests maintain themselves by providing constant circuses for children, these children may find the "bread" of live theatre very little to their taste.[11]

Children, however, do seem to feel from an early age that inherent difference between the technological image and the immediacy of the live performance. The live actors make the proceedings for them more real and less illusionary than television. Others, accustomed to the generally explicit, realistic details on the screen are sometimes baffled by symbols in the theatre as well as by minimal or expressionistic settings. Television style and vocabulary has crept into the theatre experience. Many writers have been influenced by television and the movies. They write in short, episodic scenes, frequently using flashbacks through lighting changes. Children have been heard to refer to blackouts and scene changes as "commercial breaks."

An encounter with live theatre may provoke violent physical reaction, as was reported by the Otrabanda Company, an American troupe travelling by unmotored raft on the Mississippi and playing to general audiences in a tent in small riverside communities:

> There was an incredible amount of energy expended by these spectators, especially the children, when they were addressed directly by the performer. In the second *River Raft Review* there was a feud between Mr. Ohio, the master of ceremonies, and his wife, Tootsie Ohio. Tootsie was bossed and belittled by her husband and so decided to have her own show separate from his. A contest ensued in which the audience was to be the judge. When Tootsie asked if she was doing okay so far, she was met not only with a chorus of shouts of "yes" and "no," but these shouts, whistles and screams went on and on, as if they would never stop. The children chucked bits of grass, which they pulled up in great handfuls, at the performers. The performance could not

continue for several minutes and the whole
tent full of people threatened to dissolve
into chaos. It seemed the live show was so big
and so real after television, the only entertainment most had seen before, that it threw the
young population into absolute frenzies of un-
controllable excitement and made it difficult
to perform.[12]

Another difference between television and live theatre is in form. Much of children's television consists of a series of short sketches or scenes on varying topics — more like a variety show. A theatre presentation is usually based on a script which, although it may include many different scenes, revolves around one theme. More concentration is demanded of the viewer. Most would argue as a corollary that a richer experience is the result. What makes television producers think that a continuous thirty or sixty minute story would not be entertaining? (Accommodation of commercials seems the only answer.) One cannot ignore that the most prevalent segment on television, for all ages, consists of ten minutes of concentrated time without a commercial break. There should be some other way of organizing television time, perhaps through subsidy or user support, as with the Public Broadcasting System in the United States. In some European countries, the commercials are all grouped together during each broadcast hour. A Norwegian graduate student, Stig Erikkson, in residence at the University of Calgary in 1977-78, came to Canada with a prejudice against television in his own country: he thought it boring and unimaginative. After three months in Canada with his young family and many hours of viewing a colour set, he was appalled at the intrusion of commercials here and full of admiration for his own government restricting broadcast hours to after four p.m. Two girls from Germany, Marlais Raines and Christal Drieschner, also in Calgary for the season 1977-78, found they could not bear to watch our television. In part, their aversion came from the fragmentation of programs and in part from the content of the commercials, particularly what they viewed as sexist personal hygiene and household ads.

Nat Eek, former president of ASSITEJ, World Organization

of Theatre for Children and Youth, has contrasted television with live theatre:

> As an art form it is temporal; it exists only while it continues, and once the curtain falls it ceases to exist. . . .Film is larger than the audience member, while television is smaller, but theatre approaches you on an equal basis. . . .The audience actually participates in the performance and affects its eventual success. . . .a child commenting that she liked theatre better than movies or television because the actors were "round" rather than "flat." [13]

One hopes for more enlightened uses of television; its values have been largely wasted so far on uninspiring programs for all ages.

Footnotes

1. Shamberg, Michael. "Video Literacy: Learning the Language of Television," *Horizon,* January, 1978, p. 85.
2. Lesser, Gerald S. *Children and Television,* Vintage Books, New York, 1975, pp. xxii-xxiii.
3. *The Calgary Herald.* "TV Watchers Suffered 'Withdrawal'," Friday, December 16, 1977, p. B10.
4. Mayer, Martin. "It Isn't Easy Being Educational—The Sesame Street Process," *Audience,* Volume 2, Number 2, March-April, 1972, p. 92.
5. Lesser, Gerald S., *op. cit.,* pp. 22-23.
6. Mayer, Martin, *op. cit.,* p. 92.
7. Doan, Richard K. "Kindergarten May Never be the Same Again," *T.V. Guide,* July 11, 1970, p. 8.
8. Lambert, Betty. "On Writing Plays for Children: or, You Can't See the Audience from the Trapeze," *Canadian Children's Literature,* Number 8/9, 1977, p. 29.
9. Sheilds, Roy. "We've Flipped," *T.V. Guide,* December 31, 1977, p. 6.
10. Kennedy, John, "Kids TV: Who Does it Best?" *Chatelaine,* May, 1976, p. 115.
11. Frost, Ruth, *op. cit.,* p. 24.
12. Maddou, Ellen. "The Otrabanda Company," *The Drama Review 70,* June, 1976, p. 43.
13. Eek, Nat. Closing Speech at the 5th International Congress of ASSITEJ, Berlin, East Germany, April 24, 1975.

In the Schools

The arts form a small part of the average student's education in Canada. And, among the arts, drama is the most neglected. Music and art have established more legitimacy with educators while dance and movement are components in the physical education program. Drama most often means the Christmas concert, or dramatizing incidents from stories, or Social Studies units. Exposure to live theatre is rare, often non-existent. Some enlightened principals, teachers and parents feel that theatre is important enough to warrant the occasional outing, but attending plays on a regular basis is rare for Canadian children.

Many theatres performing in schools are forced to straddle two stools : the artistic (intuitive) and the educational (verbal). Often they fall between the two. This is frustrating to many artistic directors, writers and actors. Some companies play in schools for economic reasons and are willing to compromise in order to stay in business. In Canada at the present time, a full-time professional company performing for young audiences could not survive unless it played in schools. Live theatre is not woven into the fabric of our children's everyday life and would be only a Saturday, Sunday or holiday theatre without the support of school shows. In some places, an association with education is welcome: in England, it has led to the development and phenomenal growth of Theatre-in-Education, or TIE teams. This popular movement has education through theatre as its primary goal. In TIE, the actors are also actively involved as teachers and leaders; they often include the audience as actors and problem-solvers. This is divergent from the traditional relationship where actors act and the audience observes:

> . . . . This quality of harnessing the children's
> desire to be actively involved in an experience
> created for them and with which they identify,
> by integral participation, seems to me to be the
> really significant contribution that the TIE
> movement has made to the field of theatre.
> Where the active involvement affects the course

of the play, the nature of the experience
changes.[1]

Some theatre companies would claim their objectives to be quite opposite to those of the TIE teams. Many would agree with Douglas Riske, of Alberta Theatre Projects, who states that art is his primary goal and educational achievements are secondary. Gloria Shapiro-Latham, Director of the Vancouver Playhouse Theatre-in-Education company in 1975, said:

> As I began to evolve the current Theatre-in-
> Education programme, an idea filled the air.
> It was an idea to help youth become
> involved in their communities.[2]

Social action was the primary goal of this project. This use of theatre has been frequent in the history of the art: the recent out-cropping of agit-prop players in Western Europe, the consciousness-raising plays of Marie Hébert for La Marmaille in Québec and the didactic drama of contemporary China are some examples. Such theatre is offensive to the purists.

Some Canadian companies do not make education or social action their primary objectives, but they do not mind travelling to schools. The directors of Mermaid Theatre, for example, never compromise their artistic integrity. However, the range of subjects and material may be curtailed in choosing a season which includes school tours. Mermaid does not feel resentment, but, like many companies, they are restricted by the many pipers who call their tune.

Another danger in having the professional arts linked with educational institutions is that some educators will attempt to turn experience into verbiage. If a teacher requests a specifically rigid form of critical analysis, the experience could be missed or cheapened. Isadora Duncan is quoted in the Rockefeller Report, *Coming to Our Senses*, "If I could TELL you what I mean, there would be no point in dancing." The importance of the intuitive and personal response is not well enough cherished and much of the genuine value of going to the theatre is lost:

> Explaining to a child why a fairy tale is

48

so captivating to him destroys,
moreover, the story's enchantment, which
depends to a considerable degree on the
child not quite knowing why he is delighted
by it.[3]

Doris Lessing, in the preface to *The Golden Notebook*, also talks about death by analysis:

. . . . the book is alive and potent and fructifying
and able to promote thought and discussion
only when its plan and shape and intention are
not understood, because that moment of seeing
the shape and plan and intention is also the
moment when there isn't anything more to be
got out of it.[4]

One wishes that there could be an opportunity for a company of high artistic quality to be afforded sufficient financial security to explore, experiment and produce exciting art forms without having to be accountable to the schools.

Footnotes

1. O'Toole, John. *Theatre in Education: New Objectives for Theatre—
   New Objectives in Education*, Hodder and Stoughton, London,
   1976, p. 18.
2. Shapiro-Latham, Gloria. "Planit (A Community Action Game),"
   ASSITEJ Canada Newsletter, Spring, 1976, p. 16.
3. Bettleheim, Bruno. *The Uses of Enchantment*, Vintage Books,
   New York, 1977, p. 18.
4. Lessing, Doris. *The Golden Notebook*. Panther Books, Frogmore, St.
   Alban's, Herts., "Preface," p. 22.

The Professional Theatre Person and the Child

Plays for young people have existed only since the beginning of the twentieth century. The first company to specialize in playing for the young was founded in Russia in 1917 by Natalia Sats. In the West, only since the Second World War has performing for young people become a recognizable branch of the professional theatre. Traditions and repertoire are still being established. The identity of "children's theatre" in the minds of the general public is still precarious: many people think that it means plays performed *by* children as well as *for* them. Most people do not think about the subject at all, or at best only when their own children are of an age to be diverted by spectacle, but not yet able to choose and attend entertainment on their own. The critical capabilities of a child between two and ten are limited. His reactions are fresh and impressions gained by the strong experience of live theatre are bound to be deep, important and lasting. But it is from adults, not children, that feedback on points of professionalism must come. It is from colleagues, critics and the adults in the audience that persons working in theatre for young people receive a professional self-image. And few adults are willing or able to respond sensitively to this normal artistic need.

Since theatre for young audiences has become a separate and growing business, actors' attitudes to the field are almost as varied as the individuals themselves. The actor meets the audience directly and his attitude is critical to the success of any play. Certain actors feel unappreciated when acting for the young. Jerome Ackhurst (actor in *The Clown Who Laughed and Laughed*) expresses some feelings of directors and designers as well as actors in the profession:

> Like most actors doing kid's plays, I would
> rather be doing straight dramatic roles. Only
> one in a hundred actors involved in children's
> theatre is in it because that's what he really
> wants to do. It provides experience and
> money — I do it to get away from having to
> wash cars or dig gardens for a living. I will
> probably fumble my way through one more
> production until I've gathered enough on the

business end of the theatre tó start something
in the riskier area of adult drama.[1]

Actors who play for children have both positive and negative
thoughts about the genre. For many it is just a job, often their
first. They feel that "you begin here and wait for a break in
adult theatre." Pragmatists add: "It's a booming business and
there is an opportunity for practising one's art." Sometimes
actors have formed a company and made playing for young
people a priority. Globe Theatre was one; Theatre Five in
Kingston, Ontario, is another. Reactions of many actors in
such companies are more positive. Valerie Robertson, writing
of her company's work in the *ASSITEJ Canada Newsletter*
(Spring, 1976) notes: "Another important aspect of our work is
that all the actors enjoy playing for and working with children.
All of us have been involved with children, *through choice. . . .*"
(italics ours).

In Theatre Five, the same actors perform for adults as on the
school tour. To provide weightier material for actors than the
one-act play provides is one way to increase the prestige of
acting for children. A variety of roles also helps the individual
actor to grow. Some actors, although adults, look very young
for their years. Because theatre for young people almost always
features a young hero or heroine, the demand for actors who
can play such parts is great. Some performers find themselves
in a company for young people because of their physical
appearance. A few fall in love with the genre; Barbara
Poggemiller, a seven-year veteran, is one such actress:

> I learned that to work in theatre for young
> people is to have confidence and faith in both
> director and work, to recognize my own
> strengths, to realize there are no security
> blankets. Yet I must remain vulnerable and
> sensitive. If I can't lay my emotions on the line
> as a character, then I cannot be convincing
> to anyone or stir the emotions of my
> audience.[2]

In Eastern Europe, where theatre for young people is
subsidized as matter-of-factly as the transit system, a life-time

career would await an actress as intelligent and gifted as Barbara Poggemiller. In Leningrad, an actress who first played *The Little Hunchbacked Horse* in 1922, now plays "babushkas" (grandmothers) at the Leningrad Theatre of the Young Spectator. Because the company plays for youth up to eighteen years old, this actress has performed roles from Shakespeare, Gorky and Gogol, as well as in musicals and fairy tale adaptations. If we were to create a permanent repertory company in each province of Canada whose job it was to perform for young people aged five to eighteen, we would not lack talented performers. Many would be happy to make a lifetime commitment to playing a variety of roles in a permanent company. As it is now, an ambitious performer must be prepared to move at any time on a freelance basis anywhere in the country. At the beginning of an acting career it is important above all to be *noticed*. As one young actress put it in an interview on CBC radio, when asked about playing the leading role in a Christmas production of *Winnie the Pooh*, "It was fun, but who *notices* you inside a bear-suit?"

Directors generally view a play for young people as "just another job," unless they have a special commitment toward such theatre. Most of Canada's professional theatres for young people were begun by idealistic directors. After a few years they often become discouraged as they notice other companies moving ahead in prestige, salaries and professional opportunities merely because, as far as they can see, they perform for adult audiences. When the international executive of ASSITEJ met in Alberta in 1977, some local directors declined to meet informally with theatre people and scholars from Italy, Yugoslavia, the U.S.S.R., Spain, Czechoslovakia, Cuba, Israel, Germany, Roumania and the U.S.A., claiming they did not "know anything about children's theatre." One Canadian colleague invited had directed plays for young people, successfully. When pressed he admitted that any association, *even social*, with the field, diminished his own and others' opinions of his "real" theatre work. What can one say? Is it *that* different? If it is, of course, it deserves to be criticized and we must make it better. But again one wonders if the true root of the problem is not the general attitude of society towards childhood and the rejection of the archetypal child in these "adults" which makes them so fearful, hostile and vicious in their attitude toward those who work for children.

A practical way to improve the status of the professionals would be to pay them more. Designers, for example, are often offered lower fees to design a play for children than for a similar assignment for adults. The budget allotted to the execution and supervision of the design work is frequently too small to allow a good job to be done. Pat Flood did exceptional work for Alberta Theatre Projects' junior high play, *The Devil's Instrument* by W.O. Mitchell, and for the Theatre Calgary Stage-Coach production of *Beowulf*. She says she enjoyed designing these plays, but that often the higher priority of the adult season and the much lower production budget of the young people's group meant that artistic compromises which would not have been tolerated on "the main stage" were made in the "kids' shows." Michael Maher, an award-winning designer in Ontario, created a world in which actors could move with style and distinction for Betty Jane Wylie's *The Old Woman and the Pedlar* for Young People's Theatre in 1977. He expected to design just one show, at the beginning of his professional career, for YPT. That seems to be the only time that companies performing for children can afford to hire fine designers — at the inexpensive beginning of their career. In Europe, particularly in the heavily state-subsidized theatres of Eastern Europe, no such parsimony inhibits production values. In Canada, however, most professionals receive less money, *for any service*, when they perform that service for young people.

Performances for young people are not regularly reviewed in the press or on radio or television. Canada's arts magazines carry no regular comment on them. There is no critic who specializes in theatres for young people and most critics comment upon their work only from time to time. Often the most junior stringer of the entertainment section is sent to review them. The result is that qualified appraisal is rare indeed. And continuity — the critical consummation devoutly to be wished — is woefully absent. To be fair, a part of the problem has been the great deal of second-rate and shoddy material produced for children, often by opportunists or well-meaning amateurs, sometimes by misguided or mistaken professionals. In the Soviet Union, serious criticism in this field came only when good writers wrote good plays which were then well designed and well directed by inventive and sensitive artists. Now, besides regular attention from many critics in newspapers and journals, there are about half a dozen critics of repute who are especially interested in theatre for the young spectator. It is our belief that in Canada critical assessment must catch up with the exciting progress in this genre. A few years ago, dance had no regular or special critics in Canada; now there are several. Theatre for young audiences must find similar status. It is important if professionalism is to continue to develop.

Having a home also aids professionalism. The accomplishments of Susan Rubes for her Young People's Theatre in Toronto have impressed everyone for a decade. But in opening her theatre and drama centre, the first in Canada exclusively for young people, she has set new standards for the rest of the country. It is good to have a home. If you have a hit show, you can hold it over. If you want to show a school tour to a wider public, you have a showcase at hand. Weekend performances for families will build a discriminating and responsible audience; some members of that audience will then be ready to defend the work if it is endangered. Children can begin to make going to the theatre a regular event in their lives. Susan Rubes is not the only one who believes in having a home. The late George Devine wrote in England, back in 1952:

> There must be a theatre with a particular
> policy and children must come to that theatre.
> A touring policy must finally be wrong for two
> reasons: the children themselves look on the
> theatre as a rarity, as something that comes
> from London and not part of their lives in the
> way that the weekly visit to the cinema has now
> become; and from the point of view of the
> actors, they cannot be expected to keep them-
> selves in training or to develop their abilities
> under a regime which imposes usually nine and
> sometimes ten performances a week. . .Touring
> also imposes many unsuitable theatres on the
> company.[3]

While we cannot agree that a "touring policy must finally be wrong" — in a country the size of Canada we must tour or many citizens would never experience live theatre — still the advantages of a building are many and substantial. Alberta Theatre Projects is happy to have a home base and their audiences, children and adults, have come to love the intimate surroundings of the Canmore Opera House.

The most spectacular such building in North America is the $4.5 million Minneapolis Children's Theatre, opened in 1974. Its artistic director, John Donahue, built a company of great distinction that receives support from all levels of government, along with assistance from the Rockefeller Foundation. We visited this remarkable theatre in its opening months. It is a superb facility with a classroom complex, scene and costume shops and all the essential areas of which many members of the general public are unaware. In Albany, New York, Patricia Snyder has been the power behind the creation of a special and thoroughly modern theatre building to house the Empire State Children's Theatre. In both cases, the establishment of a repertory company either preceded or accompanied the move into a permanent space. And both theatres are playing to classes (brought by buses to the theatre) as well as family audiences. We need more permanent homes for young people's theatre in Canada.

The first professional company for children in Canada was established in Vancouver in 1951 — Holiday Theatre. Today there are over forty companies whose work includes a significant number of productions especially for young audiences. If the next twenty-eight years can bring the same growth in quality and prestige that the past twenty-eight years have in quantity and opportunity, it would be a proud achievement. More permanent buildings, bigger budgets, some knowledgeable critics, mature directors and designers and more talented actors committed for a greater portion of their careers are all important ingredients. But possibly the most crucial are playwrights and we want to examine more closely their present role and the future development of a repertoire of plays for young people.

Footnotes

1. Dawson, Eric. "Clown Actor Ready to Take on Challenge of Adult Drama Fare," *The Calgary Herald*, June 10, 1977, p. 45. (Dawson Interviewed Actor, Jerome Ackhurst.)
2. Poggemiller, Barbara, quoted in "Giving Children Credit" (An Interview with the Actress by Barbara McLauchlin), *ASSITEJ Canada Newsletter*, Spring, 1978, p. 39.
3. Devine, George. "Theatre for Children: Art That Is Different," *World Theatre II*, 1952, pp. 13-14.

Repertoire and Writers

Most authors who write for both adults and children state that the only difference between the two is that one must keep in mind the limited life experience of the child. Also, a piece written for young audiences often must come between two bells in the school schedule. Therefore, the one-act play is the format most often employed. This shorter form may mean that less time is spent on development of characters, but the advantage is that a skilful author may have to pack powerful language and images into a shorter space. The one-act play has a venerable place in the adult repertoire. It is also the length that playwrights often begin with to learn their craft. Several Canadian writers have done so for young audiences and gone on to produce successful full-length plays for adults. Some authors are respectful and professional in their attitude while others distinctly dislike writing for children. In an interview in the York University *Theatre Journal*, 1974, Carol Bolt is quoted as saying: "But for me it's silly to have a review of *Tangleflags*." Why? It is disappointing to find the author of such successful scripts as *Cyclone Jack* and *My Best Friend Is Twelve Feet High* remarking that "other people doing children's theatre don't read the theatre pages." How widespread is this attitude that theatre for young audiences is somehow different from the legitimate theatre? If it is, we must work to combat it. Otherwise writers for whom this is a serious and high calling will be less and less motivated to continue. And new, young writers will not be attracted to a field they perceive as "second-class":

> If we are to have a significant body of children's
> plays in Canada, the playwright who writes for
> young audiences must become less anonymous.
> Children *may* be excused for not knowing
> about writers — but teachers themselves often
> ask actors if the play they have performed was
> made up by the troupe. Writers in this area
> have a beautiful task, but if we want to become
> known as playwrights we are forced to write for
> adults. This doesn't hurt us as writers for
> children — it is a good exercise and we may want

to do it anyway. Nevertheless, it is an indication that the public does not regard children's theatre as a first rank art.[1]

An important art form attracts serious artists; their work in turn attracts new aspirants and makes for a more respectable milieu. The erroneous idea that only simplistic subjects can be treated in this genre keeps some authors from writing for children.

A child deserves no less from the theatre than any member of society. While the repertoire may legitimately contain plays whose main purpose is entertainment, some commonly held beliefs about what "should" and "should not" appear in plays for young people need to be re-examined. One such idea is that plays for children should not be frightening. This issue is ultimately concerned with the purpose of art. Should theatre ideally confront all aspects of the human condition from the farcical to the tragic? Life is not totally idyllic for most people — and this includes the young. Many conflicting forces confront children. John Holt challenges the myth that "childhood is a time and an experience very different from the rest of life and that it is, or ought to be, the best part of our lives," saying "It is not, and no one knows it better than children. *Children want to grow up.*" Plays for children should, therefore, provide the opportunity to treat life seriously and provide more than slight, bland entertainment. Rex Deverell has said that writing plays for children has allowed him to write seriously about important issues and offer material that evokes fears and strong feelings dealt with in a unique way in the theatrical art form.

> Theatre deals with live people and a limited conflict, and anxieties and frights can always be settled in the normal critical appraisal after a performance. Thus, reality seems almost as much a part of the theatre as of all other experiences in real life. Unfortunately, television and radio can only partly counterbalance the frights they produce.[2]

Is it better for theatre to present the human condition as it is or as it should be? It is certainly tidier to present the ideal when all conflicts end in blissful resolution. It is also unrealistic. Why not be honest in treating dramatic conflict for any age group? The attitude of presenting only the ideal to children is rooted in the false and condescending notion that children are naive and that their innocence must be protected. At least some plays in a child's experience should challenge the audience to come to terms with serious issues, realistically:*

> The notion that characters in a children's play
> must be elementary is totally erroneous. The
> notion that in a children's play the writer can
> use only a completely pragmatic, readily recog-
> nizable theme is dubious.[3]

There is no justifiable reason that plays for children should be in any way slight, dull, didactic, flowery or insipid. Theatre should expand the consciousness, fill in the gulfs between people for any age group. One expects theatre to be more than slight entertainment or a story line unfolded. Let it acknowledge all people's — including children's — capacity for delight, joy and sorrow at the heights and depths of the human spirit:

> A play for children can last for only an hour or
> so and yet it wants to deal with tales and myths
> that are enormous in their scope — and then it
> needs to be put on by people who are creative,
> artistic and intelligent. Do you give a story a
> superficial treatment that deals with the main
> literary highlights, so that the kids report: "We
> saw his arrow, we saw Little John's staff. We
> saw Will Scarlett's red hair, we saw Friar Tuck,
> we saw Maid Marion (she was pretty with
> flowers in her hair), we saw the sheriff (he was
> mean looking) and then we went home. . . .?"
> Or do we take one episode or one kind of idea

---

* Joe Wiesenfeld's play "Hilary's Birthday," performed by Green Thumb Players in the Winter of 1979, caused a minor sensation in Vancouver, because it dealt realistically with the conflict between a ten year-old girl and her divorced mother's new boyfriend. *(P.H.)*

or event and flesh it out? You know that this is
a very important problem. This is what we are
trying to get at and what the Rockefeller Foun-
dation would like us to discover—how to do
good plays for young people, plays that are exciting, that have some narrative literature, that
attract the artist, that make the artist want to
become deeply involved, and that are artistically rewarding.[4]

If the purpose of art is to elicit a creative response, not all
Canadian scripts achieve this end. The challenge to face a
human crisis and to inspire imaginative insights does not come
from plays which offer neat and tidy role models in predictable
story lines.

Sometimes a performance that is so complete
at the moment that it ties up all the loose ends
and thus joins closure, may have a less lasting
effect than a less perfect performance which
leaves problems or relations unsolved in the
minds of the audience and thus sets off a continuing creative process.[5]

Nor need vocabulary, theme and conflict be simplified to
suit the lowest common denominator in the audience. It is
better that the play challenge the most mature audience
member while offering the proverbial "something for everyone." Sheila Egoff has said that "children's spoken and
listening vocabulary is far superior to their reading one." And
in the theatre, much of the meaning of lines lies in the subtext
and the action, as a visit to a play in a foreign language—save
the most static—will reveal to all but the most literally minded
audience.

Canadian scripts fall into various categories: myth, fantasy,
history, farce and realism. Some plays are participational, re-
quiring vocal or physical involvement from the audience. To
argue the "correctness" of any one genre is to focus falsely on
the problem of scripts for children. There are too few scripts of
quality in any genre. The few good scripts are soon exhausted
by companies, and the search for more is frustrating. Canada

needs to encourage good playwrights to write for young audiences just to satisfy the present appetite from season to season. One should support the local playwrights no matter what genre they choose. Some Canadians who have written successfully for child audiences include: James Reaney, Len Peterson, Eric Nicol, Betty Lambert, Betty Jane Wylie, Henry Beissel, Carol Bolt, Paddy Campbell, Rex Deverell, Dennis Foon and Jan Truss. But there are just as many other playwrights producing scripts that are fatuous, empty and unworthy of attention.

What does one expect from a good script for young people? Some meaning for the child is a good start:

> Children's playwrights are often guilty of addressing the question to the wrong party. They ask themselves what is important to children. It would be better if they asked children what is important to children. It would be better still if they asked themselves what is important to themselves. It would be best if they could join forces with the children to create a play of importance to both parties.[6]

Rex Deverell has listed some subjects he feels are important to people: home, being loved, a sense of self-worth, flight and values. His own plays show that he has practiced what he preaches. *Shortshrift* traces a town through troubled times when the inhabitants' sense of self-worth has been undermined by manipulative bureaucracy, more concerned with "efficiency" than people. Values—"How to act in our society and how to judge our own actions," as the author says—are also a part of *Shortshrift*. . . .Indeed, values come into every Deverell script. Not surprising, since he trained to be a minister. Flight figures largely in *The Copetown City Kite Crisis* and being loved is central to *Sarah's Play*. Home is important in Jan Truss's play, *Oomeraghi Oh!*, as are values and light. The traveller's tinsel and trinkets lure the family away; the brother and sister return as whispers and the smallest child remains true to the home, to which all return, more mature and less innocent.

A good play for children should challenge the child beyond

the level he has currently reached, through imagination and fantasy. It should offer moments of comfort in the recognition of similarity, understanding and compassion for others and stimulation to speculate further. A good play should enlighten its audiences about themselves. Carol Bolt's *My Best Friend Is Twelve Feet High* provides an effective mirror of the peer pressures of "exclusive clubs" and the hurtful exclusions they engender, particularly around age nine and ten. Also, Paddy Campbell's *Madwitch* shows with skill and compassion the ostracism of an old Indian woman by young children who, in their lack of understanding, are afraid of her and mock her. Betty Jane Wylie's *Kingsayer* effectively illustrates the pecking order on a school playground. Any parents who have accompanied their children to this play are reminded that only by keeping the child within them alive can they keep a relationship with their own offspring. Good plays for young people, as for any people, need to be truthful:

> This occurs when we say to ourselves of what is
> going on on stage: "I know I have never seen
> that before but I know it is true." It occurs
> when the action on stage taps the dark part of
> our imagination and becomes the mirror of our
> dreams.[7]

Poor scripts are those that are vacuous. What Bettleheim says about such stories in literature is also true of the theatre: "The worst feature of these. . . is that they cheat the child of what he ought to gain from the experience of literature: access to deeper meaning and that which is meaningful to him at his stage of development."[8] Dialogue in poor scripts is utilitarian, stilted, stale, obscure or has "hip" modernisms which can spoil the tone of the play, particularly if based upon legend or fairy tale. The humour is thin and often forced. It does not build or add to the play, but merely "gets a laugh."

Many people feel that there are topics which should be taboo in theatre for young people. Most serious writers for children, however, have included strong subjects. *Tom Sawyer* includes murder; death is never far below any but the most superficial reading of Lewis Carroll's "Alice" books, particularly *Through the Looking Glass.*

I have no patience with those who say that love
and death are not proper subjects for children.
Children can often respond to these large subjects with minds less infected than their print-
sodden elders. It is largely in childhood. . . .
that we learn of attitudes to admire, which we
can then try out in real life — the heroic, the
quixotic, the stoical, the impossibly magnani-
mous. . . .we learn from them a language of
feeling and enlarge our own vocabularies.[9]

Jonathan Levy defends the capacity of children to consider
and care about large issues and the ability of a play to be a significant event in the life of a child:

Children do not have less of a capacity to feel
than we do. Their emotions run as deep as ours
do: to the bottom. Children have less experience than we have, but they remember it
better. What's more, their imaginations are less
programmed than ours and their skins are less
thick. They can, I am convinced, be reached by
a play on this deepest level of recognition. And
when they are, they can be changed by it, as I
doubt we adults any longer can. For a child, a
play can become more than a passing entertainment, more than a vicarious adventure, more
than a walking lesson, and even more than a
parable. It can become for him the prototype,
the first formulated instance of some profound
human condition. As such, it can become part
of his very deepest experience, and remain a
point of reference in his later life.

I think all of us who work in children's theatre
should recall this every so often to keep us
serious — and I mean "serious" not as the opposite of cheerful, but as the opposite of careless
and offhand — and to keep us hopeful.[10]

Footnotes

1. Deverell, Rex. "Towards a Significant Children's Theatre," *Canadian Children's Literature*, Number 8/9, 1977, p. 18.
2. Kupper, Herbert. "Fantasy and the Theatre Arts," *Educational Theatre Journal*, March, 1951, p. 36.
3. Shwartz, Eugene. "The Most Demanding Audience," *Theatre for Children, Adolescents and Youth*, Translated by Miriam Morton, Iskvsstvo Press, 1972.
4. Donahue, John Clark and Linda Welsh Jenkins. *Five Plays from the Children's Theatre of Minneapolis*, University of Minnesota Press, Minneapolis, 1975, pp. 9-10.
5. Anderson, John. "Psychological Aspects of Child Audiences," *Educational Theatre Journal II*, December, 1950, p. 287.
6. Deverell, Rex, *op. cit.*, p. 15.
7. Levy, Jonathan, *op. cit.*, p. 11.
8. Bettelheim, Bruno, *op. cit.*, p. 4.
9. Smith, Janet Adam, compiler. *The Faber Book of Children's Verse*, Faber and Faber, London, 1972, p. 22.
10. Levy, Jonathan, *op. cit.*, pp. 11-12.

Part Two
Canadian Companies

A Very Merry Unbirthday to You

Professional theatre for children in Canada was twenty-five years old in 1978. The continuing growth in the number of companies and the expansion of repertoire, particularly new plays, is encouraging. On the other hand, the high rate of attrition, the general level of playwriting for the genre and the low regard in which work for young people is held within theatrical circles give cause for pessimism: these reflect the attitude of contemporary society toward children and childhood.

In 1977, the Stratford Shakespearean Festival of Ontario celebrated its twenty-fifth anniversary. Over fifty critics attended the marathon of openings in June. The media went mad over Stratford, which was proclaimed in New York and London as a rival to the Royal Shakespeare Company. Canadian critics were not as fulsome in their praise; even with British stars Maggie Smith and Brian Bedford gracing the season it was still, after all, our own and, therefore, suspect in genuine stature. Most Canadians though, if they thought about it at all, were no doubt pleased and proud that Stratford was celebrating its silver jubilee so successfully.

A similar landmark for professional theatre for children would have been passed and could have been celebrated in 1978 if Holiday Theatre, established by Joy Coghill and Myra Benson in Vancouver in 1953, had continued to exist. Humpty Dumpty, in *Through the Looking Glass*, instructed Alice on the advantages of "unbirthday presents":

> ". . . .and that shows that there are three
> hundred and sixty-four days when you might
> get unbirthday presents."
> "Certainly", said Alice.
> "And only *one* for birthday presents, you
> know. There's glory for you!"
> "I don't know what you mean by 'glory',"
> Alice said.[1]

We might, therefore, consider an unbirthday celebration for our theatre for young people It would be an appropriate accompaniment for the other *un's* it enjoys: an unappreciated, unnoticed, undervalued, underwritten, under-rehearsed underdog.

An investigation of the rise and fall of the Holiday Theatre, our first professional theatre for children, is of more than archival interest. This one company contained most features of the overall growth of professional theatre for the young in this country since 1953. It began, like so many Canadian arts institutions, with a colonial vision. First of all, the name — Holiday. It accurately reflects the most prevalent mode of theatre for children in the United States at the time that Joy Coghill received her training at the Goodman Theatre in Chicago. This was generally a weekend and holiday entertainment for boys and girls and their families with scripts based on fairy tales, classic children's books, historical incidents or biographies of great men. *Cinderella, Hans Brinker and the Silver Skates, The Indian Captive* and *Young Abe Lincoln* are all typical American plays of that period.

One of the great ladies of children's theatre was a teacher, director and playwright at the Goodman. She was Charlotte Chorpenning and her influence has been enormous, both as a teacher and excellent director, and as the author of the first scripts seriously written for young people in the U.S.A.[2]

The publication of the Chorpenning scripts by The Children's Theatre Press, under the dedicated editorship of Sara Spencer, meant that literate scripts by a writer with professional experience in the theatre were available to a wider public and other producers. Chorpenning's plays are out of fashion now: they seem over-didactic and static. But they were an important contribution to an infant branch of dramatic literature, and they are still performed all over the world. Some of the scripts, like *The Emperor's New Clothes,* are well-crafted, exciting versions of the classics, retaining the essence of the originals.

It was this kind of theatre that Joy Coghill and Myra Benson established with Holiday. Adaptations of fairy tales and the classics were to dominate the repertoire of Holiday Theatre until 1967.[3] Canada's Centennial celebrations included the production of many new commissioned works, among them the winner of the Holiday Theatre competition for a new play: Eric Nicol's *Beware the Quickly Who.* It, along with Betty Lambert's *The Riddle Machine,* toured the nation as part of the celebrations. Holiday was used to touring. Taking live theatre to all British Columbia children was one of its early aims. And for twenty-two years the company toured, establishing a precedent followed by almost every other theatre for young people subsequently established in Canada. For most of its life, Holiday provided two kinds of theatre: large proscenium plays for the Vancouver area and smaller touring shows for the rest of the province.

In 1969, Holiday merged with The Playhouse, Vancouver's adult regional theatre, and became Holiday Playhouse. It is more difficult to pin an exact date upon the next change of name — this time to Playhouse Holiday — but again, the name was a reflection of new reality. The power and glory that Holiday brought to the marriage had diminished with the departure of Joy Coghill to the East to head the English speaking section of the National Theatre School. The artistic leadership of both Holiday and of the Playhouse floundered and the dowry (The Playhouse cut its $50,000.00 deficit with Holiday assets in 1969) was gone.

Paxton Whitehead, then artistic director of The Playhouse, appointed Don Shipley as director of Playhouse Holiday in 1971. Shipley scheduled revivals of Holiday favourites for the first season while he conscientiously sought a new direction for our oldest theatre for the young. On a trip to England he found one about which he could be enthusiastic. With the best intentions in the world Shipley, and his immediate successor, Gloria Shapiro-Latham, launched the second wave of colonialism in Holiday's history. They changed the emphasis of production to the Theatre-in-Education (TIE) techniques of England.[4] The next and final name change occurred. Playhouse Holiday, alias Holiday Playhouse, nee Holiday Theatre became The Playhouse Theatre Centre of B.C. Theatre-in-Education. The "Holiday" was dropped completely and once more the name became an accurate reflection of reality. The new philosophy led to programs closely related to classrooms and their concerns. The large plays in the city were dropped in 1973.

Some excellent programs were devised and produced by the TIE team of The Playhouse Theatre Centre.[5] But a new set of problems emerged. Actor-teachers, the mainstay of TIE teams in England, were almost impossible to find in Canada. To train teachers to act or actors to teach was a long-range and unprecedented task. Secondly, the parent Playhouse was nurs-

71

ing a new child, a theatre school of the West, and resources over and above the subscription series were diverted there. Thirdly, the Canada Council did not recognize Theatre-in-Education as a qualifying project for federal funding because of provincial responsibility for education. Over the years the province of British Columbia had been generally supportive of Playhouse Holiday. However, in this case, the TIE teams were working mainly in Vancouver. It is easier for a provincial government to justify a province-wide tour than special services to one city. Schools (in Vancouver) had been willing to pay for two shows a day for several hundred children; they were not convinced that a team of actors working for one or more days with only thirty to sixty students gave equal value. The cost per student for a TIE team was more than most school administrators were willing to invest.

A strong touring company continued through the 1974-75 season presenting *Waterfall* by Larry Fineberg and William Skolnik, and *Paraphernalia*, an adaptation of Ken Campbell's hilarious farce, *Old King Cole*. *Waterfall* was directed by David Latham, who also had the responsibility of organizing the classes for young people offered by The Playhouse. *Paraphernalia* was directed by Gloria Shapiro-Latham, general administrator of the performance aspects of The Playhouse program for young people and artistic director of the metro TIE team. The Lathams felt that a re-examination of goals was overdue. The pressure to produce two to four plays a year, whether or not there were works they wished to put on, seemed to them to compound longstanding complaints about the limitations of the schools tour. The Lathams felt that research was badly needed, and their work with the TIE teams had encouraged them in the belief that by giving top priority to Theatre-in-Education they might discover meaningful new directions. Also, running a variety of programs—classes, schools tours and TIE teams, along with their responsibilities for artistic direction—imposed an intolerable administrative burden on the Lathams.

The last piece prepared by The Playhouse Theatre Centre of B.C. Theatre-in-Education was for teachers in Vancouver. Like all of Gloria Shapiro-Latham's experiments, it was well-received by the people for whom it was prepared. It is ironic that the last piece performed by Canada's first theatre for children was for adults only. By the 1977-78 season there was no theatre for children at all. No holiday shows for families, no tours to the interior of the province, no TIE teams. Holiday Theatre was dead. Fortunately for the children of B.C., new companies appear to be filling the old Holiday mandate of offering large productions in the city and small productions on tour. Of these the Carousel Theatre and Green Thumb Players of Vancouver and Kaleidoscope Theatre of Victoria have been particularly successful with both audiences and critics.

During its twenty-four years of metamorphoses, Holiday Theatre established the concept of professional theatre for young people, initiated the first extensive school tours of live theatre to remote areas, commissioned and performed dozens of plays by Canadian authors, and gave many young professionals their first jobs. In performing Eric Nicol's plays, *The Clam Made a Face* and *Beware the Quickly Who,* Holiday was on the crest of a new nationalism in which a distinctively Canadian script for the young was emerging. Between 1967 and 1972 there was no clear direction, but with the experiments of Gloria Shapiro-Latham, the TIE team was developing an equally distinctive Canadian content and style. We were sorry to see such an asset disappear. Both Vancouver and Canada are the poorer for it.

Two other candidates for unbirthday celebrations are the Children's Theatre of the Manitoba Theatre Centre and Les Jeunes Comédiens of Théâtre du Nouveau Monde. The latter disbanded in 1974 and apart from performances of selected plays from the adult season in schools, the Manitoba Theatre Centre has had no regular policy or special plays for young people since 1972. North America's first regional theatre was conceived with a different idea. John Hirsch and Tom Hendry wanted a populist theatre with a wide range of plays, classes for young people and a children's theatre. In the National Film Board short, *John Hirsch,* and in subsequent speeches and articles, the founders have made this commitment abundantly clear.[6] While Hirsch was artistic director, and even after he left Winnipeg for New York but remained artistic advisor, programs for young people had a vital role at MTC. Roberta Dolby directed important plays for young people; John Hirsch and Robert Sherrin staged the world premiere of James Reaney's *Names and Nicknames,* an important transitional play in Reaney's career as a playwright. David Barnett taught classes for MTC and organized a monstrous high school drama festival, where young actors acted in plays of their own, where utterly mad films were made and where the energy generated could have heated a Winnipeg winter. One constantly meets theatre people whose first brush with the stage was through David Barnett and MTC. But when the artistic director of MTC began to change every year or two, the programs for children and young people gradually disappeared. Arif Hasain, appointed artistic director in 1977, has directed and acted in plays for young people and one hopes that his leadership will mark the reinstatement of regular theatre for young audiences at the Manitoba Theatre Centre.

Les Jeunes Comédiens came out of the National Theatre School, then recently established. John Hirsch (again) and Jean-Louis Roux, director of Theatre du Nouveau Monde, thought that it would be splendid to have recent graduates of the French section of the Theatre School to form a company and perform plays in French for all of Canada. It was. The National Film Board's documentary about John Hirsch and the Manitoba Theatre Centre shows a visit by Les Jeunes Comédiens, and if one wants proof of the esprit and co-operation possible between Canada's "two solitudes," it is abundantly apparent there. One of the actresses in that film is Monique Rioux, founding director of La Marmaille, an exciting theatre for young people in Québec today. The company conducts research into appropriate repertoire for differing ages and socio-economic groups, invents ingenious dramatic games to involve entire families, and works closely with Québec playwrights.

The reasons for the demise of Les Jeunes Comédiens are not easy to assess. Maybe artistic director Jean-Pierre Ronfard was ready for a change and could not find a willing or suitable successor. In recent years, it may have been ideologically less acceptable for the young company, most of them Péquiste, to perform outside Québec. To Africa, and Europe, or Louisiana perhaps, but not for *les mauvais anglais*......

The early beginnings of professional theatre for children in Canada held much promise. There was a healthy respect within and outside the profession for the work done in the fifties by the Holiday Theatre, joined in the sixties by the

Manitoba Theatre Centre, Les Jeunes Comédiens and Theatre Hour Company.[7] It was a privilege to perform in these companies. They became the places where many young artists found their first jobs. They provided long runs, a low profile, frequent opportunity to work on classical roles (for junior and senior high school programs), new scripts (for elementary schools) and a baptism under fire in workload and endurance. Many of the artists who begin in theatre for the young do not remain there, but it is important to the future of the field that their feeling about the work should be positive. In Canada, young artists who worked with Marigold Charlesworth in the Theatre Hour Company, with Jean-Pierre Ronfard in Les Jeunes Comédiens, with John Hirsch at MTC or with Joy Coghill at Holiday Theatre took their work seriously because they were given serious work to do. Many alumni from these early companies have continued to contribute a part of their mature professional lives to theatre for young people.

One of the chief ingredients in the high quality produced by MTC and Les Jeunes Comédiens was the excellent leadership of great artists over a number of years. With a few exceptions, this calibre of leadership has been missing in our theatre for the young since. The lack has contributed to the reduced reputation of the field. Unless our few leaders of stature are recognized for the vision and dedication they bring to a generally thankless task, they too will become eligible for unbirthday presents.

Footnotes

1. Carroll, Lewis. *Through the Looking Glass*, Puffin Books, Middlesex, England, 1946, p. 274.
2. Charlotte Chorpenning did not, at least in the beginning, consider herself a playwright. She wrote her plays for young people because she could not find enough material that she wanted to produce. Much later, many directors reading Chorpenning's plays, found them less than ideal and wrote their own scripts. John Hirsch's scripts for the Manitoba Theatre Centre's early theatre for children were similarly summoned up for service by a director. Works conceived in this fashion are servicable but seem to "wear out" or "wear thin" faster than plays crafted by established playwrights. The most fruitful

combination appears to be when a director and playwright work together for several shows or seasons. Current Canadian examples include Douglas Riske and Paddy Campbell *(Under the Arch, Madwitch* and others), Riske and Bonnie LeMay *(Boy Who Has a Horse)* and Kenneth Kramer and Rex Deverell *(Shortshrift, Sarah's Play, The Uphill Revival* and others).

3. All fairy tale scripts did not come from the United States. Marge Adelberg, a B.C. playwright, was encouraged by Holiday Theatre to write adaptations of fairy tales. While Chorpenning scripts do appear in early Holiday seasons, Adelberg adaptations are as numerous. Bastion Theatre has also produced many Adelberg scripts.

4. Theatre-in-Education in Great Britain has both admirers and detractors, but its impact in the past ten years cannot be denied. A good account of its brief history, along with a discussion of its philosophical principles can be found in *"Theatre in Education: New Objectives for the Theatre—New Techniques in Education"* by John O'Toole. A colourful critic of TIE is Ed Berman, arts entrepreneur and animateur, who said to the author in an interview in October, 1972, "That animal known as TIE is something I'm reasonably unsympathetic to, and I say reasonably because I think it's rather detrimental to the growth of children. . . .An industry has grown up in Great Britain called 'theatre in education'. . . .It's totally dominated by the educational system because that's all that can in theory afford to pay for work with children."

5. For a detailed description of one of the Playhouse Centre's TIE team creations see "Planit: A Community Action Game" by Gloria Shapiro-Latham in the *ASSITEJ Canada Newsletter*, Spring, 1976.

6. In a speech to the Canadian Child and Youth Drama Association in Hamilton, Ontario in 1970, Hirsch spoke eloquently about the obligation of adult artists to present live theatre of a high quality to young people. He also talked about his own change of heart and mind about the materials appropriate for the young. At MTC in the early days, he said, he believed that the plays should be primarily fun; scripts like his own *Box of Smiles* exemplified this belief. Now, he said, having lived in New York City for some time and therefore having been forced to re-evaluate the effects of modern living upon morality, he had come to believe that theatre was a place for deeper messages. The young he thought, were looking for spiritual sign-posts. Perhaps, he suggested, adults after the second world war had wanted to "spare" the next generation the more serious side of life with its attendant anguish. And perhaps it had been this benevolent paternalism which had led eventually to the mindless and superficial fare for the young which invades North American households through TV. He recommended that directors of theatres for children not copy this trend, but serve main courses as well as desserts.

7. Theatre Hour Company was established in 1963 by Donald and Murray Davis to bring live theatre to Toronto high school students. Later, the tours were extended to all of Ontario. It is now a part of

Toronto Arts Productions, still touring Ontario's secondary schools successfully. It has seldom enjoyed a continuity of artistic direction and has not, therefore, developed a distinctive style, but it has benefited from being in the middle of English Canada's largest talent pool. This, along with directors like Marigold Charlesworth, has helped to keep the standard of production high.

Two Troupes from the Middle Years

Theatre for young audiences grew slowly in the sixties, with two or three new companies appearing each year. It gained momentum with the encouragement of the regional theatre network and exploded in the early seventies when federal funds from "make-work" programs, Opportunities for Youth (OFY) and Local Initiatives Projects (LIP) created several important theatres for young people. Also, an increased awareness by many school administrators of the value and uses of drama has built a more hospitable climate toward theatre for young people.

Many young people who started companies for children under the OFY summer employment program were idealistic in their aims, but innocent of practical experience. Some were cynical and produced plays for children merely as a meal ticket. After all, there are a lot of kids and a lot of schools and you could usually convince a few principals to hire you — once. The high standards of performance set by Canada's early theatre for children companies were seldom equalled in this rapid proliferation. And established professional theatres resented competition from free performances, subsidized by grants without regard to quality. With cutbacks in the federal programs most of these neophyte companies disappeared. But they leave behind a legacy of some slipshod work which the survivors still have to live down. Two responsible and important survivors of LIP-engendered companies, ATP and Mermaid Theatre, warrant separate study in this book.

The growth in the number and scope of adult professional companies in Canada during the sixties was even more remarkable. But, except for growth and rapid expansion, there are more differences than similarities between theatre for adults and theatre for children in this country. It may be helpful to remind ourselves of the main differences between the two before we examine more closely two important companies, each into a second decade of service: Young People's Theatre of Toronto and Globe Theatre of Regina, Saskatchewan.

In most regional theatres a "balance" between comedy and serious plays, classics and contemporary pieces and new Canadian works is an unwritten guideline for choosing a season. In a company performing for children, although the style may differ from one company to the next, each company usually stays primarily within one style. Adult companies present full-length plays from ninety minutes to three and a half hours long. Companies for children tend to present one-act plays lasting from forty to sixty minutes. An adult company often has a permanent building and performs primarily in that one location. A company for children is usually a touring company. An adult company works with various sizes of casts.[1] In companies performing for children the standard is between four and six players. Adult professional companies in most Canadian cities receive regular reviews and serious criticism. Productions for young people are given sparse notices by reviewers either jejune or jaded. There is little continuity in the critical vantage point. An adult professional company employs actors of all ages and degrees of experience. When we look at theatres for young audiences we find that almost all actors are young, with little or no experience. Finally, audiences for the adult theatre choose to attend: they buy their tickets for the show or the season. The audiences for children's theatre are largely captive: children do not buy their own tickets, but attend a play either as a part of school or are taken to the theatre by parents who have purchased tickets for them.

And what kind of theatre has emerged as a result of small touring companies with young, inexperienced actors presenting one-act plays in one style to captive audiences? In 1966, two professional companies were established in Canada whose sole purpose was to present plays for young people. They are both very much alive and each has had, in its own way, a profound effect upon future developments of theatre for the young in Canada. The Globe and Young People's Theatre share many attributes, but more often their artistic styles are as far apart as the physical distance which separates them in Canada.

Looking closely at YTP and the Globe may illuminate both the strengths and weaknesses in Canada's theatre for young people. Problems of the Saturday show, the school tour, repertoire and reputation are predictably present in both companies. Both have influenced many newer companies to emulate their style. With the death of the pioneering companies, the Globe and YPT now have seniority; at age thirteen, they are almost senior citizens.

Footnotes

1. Economic restrictions and inflation have made large cast shows increasingly difficult for professional theatres, but most still attempt at least one "big" show a season.

Inook and The Dandy Lion:
Young People's Theatre of Toronto

Help me, O Spirits
I am a shadow
in a land of shadows
The wind plays with me
the moon plays with me
I am fair game for the dark.
Help me become a man.[1]
from Inook and the Sun

There's nothing to it
When you know how to do it
And you know how to do it right!
Any old clown
In any old town
Knows that you start with white![2]
from The Dandy Lion

When Young People's Theatre visited England for an engagement at the Unicorn Theatre for Children in 1975, *The Observer* and *The Stage and Television Today* referred to the company as "Canada's foremost children's theatre company." Although many in Canada might dissent, it is difficult to refute the epithet. One cannot talk for very long about theatre for the young in Canada without referring to some aspect of the work done by YPT or its founder, producer and publicist extraordinaire, Susan Douglas Rubes.

Growth has been impressive. In a "Statement of Purpose" dated November 23, 1973, Susan Rubes pleads for "a home of her own" and cites impressive statistics to justify the need for a performing arts centre for the young in Toronto:

Young People's Theatre has grown in eight
years from a staff of professional artists,
instructors, technicians, administrators,
numbering eight and playing to an audience of
11,000 — to a staff of professional artists,
instructors, technicians, administrators
numbering sixty during a season and a yearly
attendance figure exceeding 200,000...

V. Tony Hauser

Susan Douglas Rubes, founder and producer of Young People's Theatre of
Toronto

84

Planning, persistence and impatience finally resulted in YPT securing a thirty-year lease on an historic building at Front and Frederick Streets, owned by the Toronto Transit Commission, but unused since 1929. Despite problems of gargantuan proportions in renovation — an expensive pumping system was made necessary when unexpected portions of Lake Ontario appeared under the floor — the new theatre opened its doors in December, 1977.

Susan Rubes arrived in Toronto from New York with her husband, singer Jan Rubes, and their three small boys in 1960. Née Susan Douglas, she left a solid career as an actress on stage, in television and radio when she moved. She had played leading roles in Broadway shows like *He Who Gets Slapped,* directed by Tyrone Guthrie, and won the Donaldson Award for Best Supporting Performance. In television, she had acted in such early drama series on American television as *Studio One* and the *ABC Playhouse,* and on radio she had played Cathy in "The Guiding Light" for ten years.

There was no professional theatre for children in Toronto, so Rubes started one. Michael Hanlon described the founding of the Toronto Museum Children's Theatre in a 1965 weekend magazine article, referring to Susan Rubes as a "fairy godmother" going out among "the chorus of angels rattling a sterling silver cup and fifty women drop a total of $5,000.00 into it." She and co-producer Brian Merriman cleared $1,200.00 in pure profit on their first venture of *Alice in Wonderland.* There followed *Sleeping Beauty* and others, including *The Dandy Lion,* which played to near-capacity crowds for five months in Toronto. A French version *(Le Lion Distingué)* "was an absolute bomb," as Hanlon mockingly remarked, "and the all-women Toronto Museum Children's Theatre lost its Pucci overblouse on it." The tone of the article, though written before the flowering of the various liberation movements in the late sixties, is nevertheless fairly typical of the stance adopted by many, especially men, about artists who devote themselves to work for children.

Such attitudes may account for some of the extra ergs Rubes uses in her long and tireless battles for her Young People's Theatre in particular and theatre for young people in general. Friends call it energy; the less friendly, chutzpah or pushiness, but anyone who has been around children's theatre for any length of time knows the need for belligerency against the inane and often insulting attitudes toward this particular contribution to culture.

Young People's Theatre came later and had a wider mandate than the Museum Children's Theatre. Plays continued to be presented on weekends and holidays in theatres, but there would also be plays to go into the schools, so as many children as possible might be introduced to live theatre by the best professional talent available. The first season a double bill of Chekhov went to junior high schools. the 1967-68 season added a play for grades 4-6; the 1968-69 season, for grades 1-3; and since 1969-70, plays for each age group have been offered, later in multiple companies.

For the Saturday and holiday shows Susan Rubes usually stayed with her first style: bright mini-musicals reminiscent of Broadway, from where she came. From the earliest years of the company she has also drawn professional writers like Dodi Robb, Pat Patterson and Chris Wiggins to write plays for her theatre. These plays are short and seasoned with slapstick. Written with craft and authority, they hold but do not touch the audience deeply. In their introduction to *The Popcorn Man,* Dodi Robb and Pat Patterson explain how they set about their task:

> When you write a play for children, you must
> bring to it the same amount of care and
> theatrical skills with which you approach a play
> for their elders. You must use everything you
> have ever learned about the craft of
> entertainment — how to create a character,
> sustain a mood, milk a laugh, and even how
> many pratfalls make one too many.
> Incidentally, we find that falls, trips and chases
> are always helpful in keeping a young audience
> entertained — particularly if the person who
> comes a cropper is an adult![3]

And Nathan Cohen had this to say about *The Dandy Lion* in *The Toronto Star:*

> *The Dandy Lion* was a show young boys and

The Popcorn Man *by Dodi Robb and Pat Patterson, one of the early successful musical scripts commissioned by YPT*

girls could respond to, ebullient and tantalizing
enough to satisfy their imagination and never
instructional, in the bad sense, or precious. . . .
What impresses this adult, aside from the
story's buoyancy and simplicity, is the professionalism of the performance.[4]

Mini-musicals like *The Dandy Lion* and Robb and
Patterson's other commissioned musicals, *The Popcorn Man*
and *Little Red Riding Hood,* are the sort of plays many adults
expect to see when they take their children to the theatre. As
produced by Susan Rubes, the high degree of professionalism
mentioned by Nathan Cohen seldom flagged.

When YPT began its schools' programs, the fare was more
controversial and more demanding of its audience. Slavomir
Mrozek's one-act play *Out at Sea,* in which the occupants of a
lifeboat attempt to eat one another, would have been at home
in an avant-garde repertoire in 1968 when YPT took it into
Ontario's junior high schools. Similarly with Jean-Claude Van
Itallie's "The Interview" from *America Hurrah,* an abrasive
and acute observation of North American life in the sixties.

And for the elementary schools, Susan Rubes produced the participation plays of Brian Way. Fairy tale adaptations and mini-musicals are not the only examples of colonialism in Canadian theatre for young people. Another such influence has been Brian Way and the participation play from England. If anything, Brian Way was the more influential upon more companies — and for several reasons. Way toured Canada twice, in the late fifties and early sixties. His charismatic and dynamic personality, coupled with his deeply felt philosophy, could not fail to impress anyone. His energy and accomplishments are remarkable. He has written over fifty plays for young people. He founded and directed the Theatre Centre until 1976. His tours were important to the education of a generation of British school children. Anyone in Canada who became interested in theatre for young people was likely to be drawn to Brian Way and his Theatre Centre in London.

There are fads and fashions in theatre for young audiences as there are in all else. The participation play was seized upon by many as "the" way, not just Brian's way, to present plays for children. The plays were attractive to hard-headed boards watching theatre expenses. Because Brian Way believed in a close relationship between child and actor, in an open rather than a proscenium stage, because his company was touring England and Canada needed touring companies to reach its widely scattered population, the participation play with its small cast, played in the round without scenery and with minimal props and costumes, seemed an attractive alternative to more expensive, traditional productions. Making necessity into a virtue, five actors with ten hats in the middle of a school gymnasium was held to be the only appropriate way to present live theatre for children. For some individuals and companies, who came to Way's philosophy fourth or fifth hand, the fact that they had to travel in a small van to remote areas itself became a philosophical statement. Of course, others used their imagination and talents to overcome the conditions of poverty which were the rule rather than the exception.

The rights to Brian Way's plays were difficult to obtain. Permission was only granted if the company agreed to limit audiences to 250 children, to perform on the open stage and to provide a director familiar with Way's theories and methods.[5]

Young People's Theatre did secure the rights to Brian

Way's plays, and produced six of them between 1966 and 1970. Four were for schools: *On Trial, The Decision, The Clown* and *The Bell.* Two were "in-theatre" productions: *The Mirror Man* and *The Dog and the Stone.* It is odd to find a revival of *The Dandy Lion* sharing a spot with *The Dog and the Stone* in the same season. Dodi Robb and Pat Patterson held views on audience participation different from those of Brian Way:

> Each play includes one or two songs which purposely invite active audience participation, such as hand-clapping or joining in a repetitive phrase. This, frankly, is a method of giving the children a chance to let off steam now and then. We respect them as an audience, but we know they are still squirmers.
>
> Another device we use for the same purpose is the establishment of one or two points in the play where the audience can shout back and forth with the actor, *in the illusion that they are helping him.* (Italics ours.) This can be simple as "Which way did he go? or "Who did it."[6]

There is nothing worse according to Way and his followers than token participation. "Which way did he go?" is considered the ultimate "dirty trick" in participation theatre — and a cop-out:

> However, we never ask our audience to create the play for us by pretending they are trees or waves or walls, or by deciding how the play shall end. These techniques are invaluable in the "creative drama" situation of classroom or workshop, but we feel that the theatre is neither a classroom nor a workshop — it is a unique artistic experience in which the audience and the players have their separate and distinct roles.[7]

It is Susan Rubes' pragmatic philosophy, as well as her excellent business acumen, which accommodate these

Androcles and the Lion *by Aurand Harris, a popular script from the United States done by YPT in commedia dell' arte style*

Inook and the Sun *by Henry Beissel*

opposites. She is an impressario, not an artistic director. If a new trend is good, she will try her hardest to find a director who knows how to do a script of that sort. Her taste has been honed during years in the business and from an eclectic sampling of theatre in Toronto and New York. She admits that she "borrowed" when YPT first began:

> Ours is a young country accustomed to borrowing from older cultures, and a decade ago there was little in Canadian theatre to warrant the term "indigenous." Young People's Theatre, understandably, began with borrowed and established works. But simultaneously, a policy of playwright development was instituted. We brought experienced professional Canadian writers from other media into the theatre, and at the same time aided and groomed the young, inexperienced writers whom training and opportunity could turn into playwrights. YPT has given dozens of commissions, and several of the resulting Canadian plays (notably *The Dandy Lion* and *The Popcorn Man* by Dodi Robb and Pat Patterson, *Inook and the Sun* by Henry Beissel and *God is Alive and Well and and Living in Heaven* by Ron Singer) have gone on to productions in Britain and the United States — returning the old favour, as it were.[8]

There continues to be some schizophrenia in the YPT scheduling of plays between the "in-theatre" and the "in-school" programs. During the 1976-77 season, for example, the "in-theatre" show was Aurand Harris' *Androcles and the Lion,* a play in the style of the *commedia dell' arte,* in which conventions like masks, slapsticks, and chases abound, It is a light-hearted romp, excellent in its genre but not particularly thought-provoking or demanding of its audience. In the schools, YPT was presenting two new plays by Caroline Zapf. In *Simre the Dwarf* the action is centred on Simre's struggle with a group of children over being different. When the children tease him too far, Simre pours them magic tea distort-

91

The Day Jake Made Her Rain *by W. O. Mitchell, a play about prairie drought in the 1930's, was designed by Peter Blais at YPT to emphasize elements of fantasy*

Maurice *by Carol Bolt*

ing their features so that they realize that "ugly" is a relative concept. And in *The Players and the King's Servant*, the action centres on stories which are used by three players against the arrogant and selfish King of Nol. In effect, the village players come to teach a despotic king a fatal lesson.[9] In this powerful play, which toured grades 4-6 in Ontario and later in Bermuda, the players kill the king on stage during the performance. The actors reported that most audiences believed it to be unfortunate, but necessary and proper that a despot should die. Who can be a "Dandy Lion" in a place like this? The dichotomy points out one of the advantages (there are lots of disadvantages, but of those, more later) of performing in schools. Teachers, in general, have a realistic idea of the subject matter and modes of presentation which young people are able or willing to absorb.

Sid Adilman, columnist for *The Toronto Star*, wrote about the erroneous ideas some adults have about children's capacity to understand strong theatre pieces. In a news item about the initiation of a special series of after-school drama by Canadian writers on CBC-TV, he discusses the first production in the new series, Len Peterson's *Almighty Voice*:

> Delegates at a recent children's television con-
> ference in Ottawa previewed the program and
> while praising it, some programmers felt it
> might be too strong for young audiences.
>
> This shows how out of touch they are with their
> audiences. *Almighty Voice* had toured Metro
> schools to the applause of children and their
> teachers.[10]

Since 1970, the schools' shows of YPT have been almost exclusively scripts by Canadian writers, many of them commissions. Playwrights included Len Peterson, Eric Nicol, Ron Singer, Larry Fineberg, Carol Bolt, Des McAnuff, Michel Gélinas, W.O. Mitchell, Larry Zacharko, Henry Beissel and Betty Jane Wylie. Most companies which present new works form a relationship with one or two playwrights over a period of years. From such collaboration a distinctive style begins to emerge. It happened at the Tarragon Theatre between Bill Glassco and

David Freeman or David French, at the Centaur Theatre with Maurice Podbrey and David Fennario, at Alberta Theatre Projects between Douglas Riske and Paddy Campbell or John Murrell and at Globe Theatre with Ken Kramer and Rex Deverell. Something of that same relationship may be seen in the works Carol Bolt created for YPT and the three early musicals by Robb and Patterson. But, because Susan Rubes is a producer not a director, the same kind of nurturing is not possible. However, one strength of the YPT has been the number of new playwrights it has encouraged and its effective campaign to have the scripts published.

Young People's Theatre has made a huge contribution in Canada. It is easily the largest operation of its kind in the country. It has produced school shows, theatre shows, French shows and experimental shows. It has run classes for kids — currently, and for the past three years, taught by the talented young men of the Homemade Theatre. It has invited companies to perform under its auspices: Company One, the Vellemen's Canadian Puppet Festival, Mermaid Theatre, to name a few. It has launched the career of dozens of actors, including John Hamelin, Diane Stapely, Bartley and Margaret Bard, and Grant McGowan. And YPT has enjoyed generally supportive press in Toronto.

Susan Rubes now has her building and that dream has become a reality. She has been generous to young Canadian artists in offering opportunities to write and to perform. It would be interesting to see what might happen if one or more young directors were to take up residencies of two or three years at the new centre. It has been pretty much a one-woman operation for ten years, as far as artistic direction is concerned. One hopes that the resources of YPT will allow the same kind of time for the development of new scripts and the rehearsal of new plays that was possible in the halcyon days of LIP. Among the most interesting pieces produced by YPT were those which evolved under the more leisurely conditions allowed by a $43,000.00 LIP grant in the early 1970's.[11] Susan Rubes has a good track record in the discovery of new playwrights. The plays written for her are head and shoulders above most others in the field, though sometimes below other works by the same playwrights. Rick Salutin's *Money* is one example; Carol Bolt's *Tangleflags* is another. This may be partly due to the restrictions placed on the author, such as the size of cast and length of play. But time on regular salary to rewrite during rehearsals and after the first run, as well as a chance to work with the same director and the same company over several years, might produce truly fine scripts with a distinct and distinguished company style.

Footnotes

1. Beissel, Henry. *Inook and the Sun,* Playwright's Co-op, Toronto, 1974, p. 27.
2. Robb, Dodi and Pat Patterson. *The Dandy Lion,* New Children's Drama 2, new press, Toronto, 1972.
3. Ross, Dodi and Pat Patterson. "Introduction" to *The Popcorn Man,* new press, Toronto, 1972, p. iii. (The same Introduction also appears in the new press edition of *The Dandy Lion* by the same authors.)
4. Quoted in the 1971-72 eight-page promotional brochure of Young People's Theatre.
5. Rights to perform Brian Way's plays in Canada were with his agent and former colleague, Margaret Faulkes Jendyk, until 1977, when Baker's Plays of Boston took over North American publication and distribution.
6. Robb, Dodi and Pat Patterson, *op. cit.,* p.v.
7. *Ibid.*
8. Rubes, Susan. "One Decade at a Time", *ASSITEJ Canada Newsletter,* Spring, 1976, pp. 13-14.
9. Plot summaries are snatched here from the hand-out sheets of YPT, distributed to teachers whose classes attend the plays and containing preparation and follow-up suggestions as well as plot summaries.
10. Adilman, Sid. "Eye on Entertainment," *The Toronto Star,* November 10, 1975
11. Ron Singer was billed as artistic director. A student company was formed and a half-dozen experimental projects generated within a two year period.

Next Town Nine Miles: Globe Theatre of Saskatchewan

> We are all marked by the first world that meets
> our eyes, carrying it with us as a permanent
> image of the way things are, or should be. My
> world was flat and open. There were no "pros-
> pects" on the prairies — only one prospect, the
> absolute, uncompromising monotony of those
> two parallel infinities, earth and sky. I draw it
> in my mind's eye, with a ruler — road and tree,
> farmhouse and elevator, all spare and simple
> and hard-edged, with a line of telephone poles
> slicing the distance. Movement in this land-
> scape has no more consequence than the leap of
> a jackrabbit across a dusty road. The stillness is
> the reality. The sounds of the prairie only
> deepen its loneliness — cowbells clinking in the
> dust, the curious thrilling hum of telephone
> wires, a coyote's yelp. Sometimes at night we
> heard the long low whistle of a train, saw the
> lighted snake as it rushed out of one mystery to
> another. Faces at the windows, dining car
> napery. . . .Its passing left us more solitary than
> ever. To grow up on the prairies is to acquire
> inevitably the image of man as a lonely travel-
> ler, moving through a universe neither hostile
> nor friendly but only infinitely remote.[1]

Fredelle Bruser Maynard writes of a Depression childhood in
Saskatchewan, but her words evoke the atmosphere also in the
best of the later prairie plays. Actors who have undergone what
is almost universally regarded as an "initiation" into professional theatre in Canada — the school tour — will also feel
ripples of recognition in the recollections of *Raisins and
Almonds*. "Absolute, uncompromising monotony" and "loneliness" or "solitary" are phrases that are bound to occur in any
extended conversation with Canadian actors who have ever
been on a school tour.

Globe Theatre of Regina, Saskatchewan, is one of
Canada's oldest professional theatres for children and was
founded expressly to take participation plays into the schools.

Ken and Sue Kramer, co-founders of Globe Theatre of Saskatchewan

Most Canadian companies tour and many are famous for one or more aspects of the touring: for example, Citadel-on Wheels/Wings of Edmonton fulfills a mandate to present theatre to remote northern communities in Alberta. Notable aspects of other companies are discussed elsewhere in this book. By studying Globe Theatre in some detail, it is hoped that several separate threads which weave through the fabric of theatre for the young in Canada — the participation play, the addition of an adult season, development of local themes and indigenous authors — can be focused. The continued and unbroken artistic direction of the company by its founders serves a function similar to that of a "control" in scientific experiments. It is also, of course, a rare attribute in a field where turnover and transience contribute to the flimsiness of philosophy, the lack of conviction and the quixotic, uninformed or irrational choices of repertoire which too often characterize theatre for children in Canada.

Ken and Sue Kramer* came to Canada in the mid-sixties with a dream. They had met at Brian Way's Theatre Centre in

*Sue Kramer died suddenly of cancer in November, 1978. Her loss at the age of 39 has been mourned by the entire theatre community in Canada. This chapter was written before this tragic event. *(P.H.)*

London and married on a school tour. After absorbing Way's philosophy through participation in his company as actors and directors, the Kramers were filled with missionary zeal

Canadian-born Ken returned home in 1965 with his British-born wife, Sue, to ride the crest of a wave of enthusiasm for child drama, creative dramatics and the participation plays of Brian Way. Because of their first-hand knowledge of Way's techniques and their own infectious energy and ability to present these dramatically, the young Kramers were in demand as speakers and workshop leaders. But their dream of establishing a professional theatre company for children in Canada, using Way's plays and principles, eluded them for nearly two years. Their first attempts to put their plans into action were in Vancouver, where Canada's oldest professional theatre for children seemed a logical place to begin.

At that time, Holiday Theatre was doing proscenium plays with no participation to audiences of 1,000 to 1,500 children. The management of Holiday was worried about trying to change a budgeting system which had been successful with the school board. They agreed to let the Kramers conduct, under the Holiday umbrella, an "experimental season"; the money would have to be raised by them from additional sources. "It just didn't seem worth the effort at the time."

So the Kramers moved next to Edmonton, Ken's old hometown. It was not sentiment, however, which dictated the move. Under the pioneering persistence of Bette Anderson, the City of Edmonton Parks and Recreation Department had initiated and maintained for many years a winter series of community theatre for children and a free summer parks program, the Playground Players. But attempts to establish a company by working from within the system (Ken was employed by Parks and Recreation) were unsuccessful. The bureaucracy was difficult to penetrate. Keen supporters of professional theatre in Edmonton were engaged in helping to establish an adult company—The Citadel. And the amateur theatre for children in the city had been of a sufficiently high standard to satisfy current public demand.

When Sue left for a summer teaching job in Charlottetown, the separation jolted the discouraged Kramers into a reassessment of their position. They had been in Canada for a year. They had made many professional contacts through their trips and workshop assignments. They had been encouraged by the enthusiasm of individuals and groups for Brian Way's methods. But their dream of a professional theatre for children based on these ideas was as far away as ever.

They decided to make one last try. Ken wrote a letter to everyone he had met in Canada in the past year:

> We had a particular style of children's theatre that we wanted to do—that we did not want to compromise it in any way—that people by this time knew what we had to offer and if anybody wanted it, they had till the middle of August to take it, otherwise we were going back to England. And lo and behold, the next day I got a telegram from Regina saying, "Would you come and talk to the Arts Board!" And I came here and we sat down with George Shaw, Executive Director of the Arts Board. And he liked the idea. And then we went and talked to the Department of Education and they liked the idea. Two weeks later we had a grant of three thousand dollars and we moved.[2]

Three thousand dollars does not sound like much now, but it seemed "an inordinate amount of money" to the Kramers at the time:

> We were incredibly naive. And I think it was a lucky accident that we did it the right way here. Because what we did here was—we did no politicking; we did no writing of briefs; we did nothing when we came here except to rehearse. And at the end of four weeks, we had three shows, fully costumed, and we had the props and everything ready to go, but we had no bookings. But our three thousand dollars paid for rehearsal costs, paid for the costumes and then we had a very tangible product that we could take to people instead of trying to describe what we wanted to do, we could take it and say, "This is it." [3]

"It" was three Brian Way plays: *The Dog and the Stone,
The Rescue* and *Shakespeare's Characters as Living People.*
The names of members of the company for the first year are of
more than historical interest: Sue Richmond, Ken Kramer,
Miriam Newhouse, Paddy Campbell, Bill Hugli and Russ
Waller (replaced later that year by Douglas Riske.) For these
actors, the first Saskatchewan season was not "just a job." It
was a mission. Miriam Newhouse has since worked with Brian
Way and has continued to serve theatre for young people with
distinction in both Canada and England. Russ Waller was devoted to the Kramers and their philosophy. He was that rare
phenomenon on school tours—a mature actor—and reminis-
cences of the first company always include mention of the
warm rapport Russ had with the first school audiences. The
terrible trial of touring on the prairie took its toll, however,
and Russ reluctantly withdrew from the company for reasons
of health. To take his place, the Kramers engaged a young actor whose work they knew from the Playground Players in
Edmonton, Douglas Riske. Paddy Campbell's and Douglas
Riske's contribution to Canadian theatre for young people is
fully chronicled elsewhere in this volume, but it is interesting to
note that, like the Kramers, they met and married through
children's theatre and the school tour. And the influence of
Brian Way and the participation play was a powerful ingredi-
ent in their early productions for the Arts Centre Theatre
Company, which preceded ATP in Calgary.

Despite a dedicated company with unshakable faith in its
principles, Globe Theatre's first season was not without
crises. The first problem was to attract bookings. People rarely
demanded a product whose properties were unknown. In a
province where live professional theatre had been absent for a
generation, it was difficult to convince people that plays were
important experiences for school children. Early performances
were presented for "whatever a school would pay"—and it often was not much. To maintain an Equity company at even minimum salaries put a great strain on the small subsidy from the
Saskatchewan Arts Board. At one point, the strain was too
much for bureaucracy to bear:

> One day we went into a bank to cash our
> cheques and they all bounced. So, we got back

to Regina and George (Shaw) met us there and
said we'd gone way beyond the amount of
money he was supposed to give us, and the Arts
Board had said "No more money—we can't
afford to do this—we've got auditors—we have
to be accountable, too." And we had another
week's bookings, and we pretty well put it to the
company—and we said, "Okay, we can either
quit now—or we can work next week and get
this week's money." And everybody said, "let's
go." So we did that extra week and then we
folded.[4]

The company "folded" twice that first season—but never
gave up. They asked for, and received, moral support from the
public for whom they played: letters from boys and girls who
had seen the plays and loved them inundated Premier
Thatcher's office. A "Catch-22" nearly wiped out government
subsidy on two levels at one point. The Canada Council pro-
mised support if the provincial government subsidized the
company; the province had no more money to give. Only a
series of personal phone calls, from George Shaw and Ken
Kramer to André Fortier, explaining that Saskatchewan did
believe in the company's work and promising in the following
year's budget a more realistic subsidy, convinced the Canada
Council that their own aid was legitimate. Also, the company
could not have survived if it had not been for the enlightened
and energetic support of a band of dedicated people who
worked in various ways behind the scenes. In addition to
George Shaw, Cal Abrahamson, Rhena Howard and Joyce
Wilkinson were among many who believed in Globe since
its inception. In 1976, Florence James received the Diplôme
d'honneur from the Canadian Conference of the Arts. In presenting it to her, her old friend, Donald Wetmore, former Arts
Advisor to Nova Scotia, cited her successful efforts on behalf of
Globe Theatre at its inception as an outstanding contribution
to Canadian theatre history.

The program the Kramers took to the Saskatchewan schools
was new to Canada, but it was not Canadian. For six seasons
Globe toured scripts by Brian Way. It is impossible to run
out of this material because Way has written over four dozen

participation plays for various age groups, and given the fact that the school population in any age group changes every three years, a new "generation" is theoretically ready to receive recycled material at regular intervals. Except for some "original arrangements" of classics devised by Ken Kramer for Division III (junior and senior high schools), no attempt was made in the early years to develop local, regional or national material. In the light of their later commitment to all three as their adult theatre emerged, and given the current obsession in some quarters with Canadian content, the exclusive use of Brian Way's plays for six seasons may seem strange. Three reasons emerge as the most important for the lack of new plays and playwrights in Globe's early school tours.

In the first place, it must be remembered that when the Kramers founded Globe Theatre, the only participation scripts available were by Brian Way. They were not only scripts; they were the embodiment of a new philosophy of drama education and theatre for children. This is a fact forgotten by many later critics who (with some justice) question the literary merit of many plays in the Way canon. Through his work with Peter Slade, his own experience as a professional actor and his observations and teaching of children, Brian Way became convinced that a more direct way must be found to present plays to young people. From this belief came the form and the style of his scripts:

1. They should be presented on an open stage or on a flat floor: the proscenium was rejected as an inappropriate and alienating form for young children.

2. The content and length of the plays should be dictated by developmental data on the growth of the child, physically, intellectually and emotionally.

3. And there should be opportunities for the child to participate actively in the development and action of the play.

Clown I, a Brian Way participation play on tour in Saskatchewan in 1969

Whether or not one agrees with this philosophy, the enormous impact it has made in the areas of drama education and theatre for children cannot be denied. And in Canada, it was the Kramers who spread the word.

Like many missionaries and converts, the letter as well as the spirit of the law was exactly followed. The story that the company warm-ups in the early days were performed to the accompaniment of the chant: "Brian Way is 'the' Way" is probably apocryphal, but it is a true reflection of the directors' devotion.

Secondly, it was a coup to stage Brian Way's plays in Canada in the mid-sixties. Well aware that his methods could be misunderstood and misinterpreted, Brian Way demanded many safeguards before granting the performing rights to his scripts. One of these was the assurance that the piece would not be played to more than two hundred and fifty persons. This limited box office receipts in a commercial theatre but was essential to achieve the participation goals of the plays. For companies operating in orthodox theatres the requirement of an open stage proved an insurmountable barrier. Finally, because he gave great attention to the special training of actors to encourage and control participation at the Theatre Centre in London, Way wanted some assurance that similar attention would be paid by Canadian companies. Not many directors in Canada were qualified to give this training. The number of actors with experience and expertise in the method could be counted on the fingers of one hand. And they were at Globe Theatre in the first company.

Thirdly, Ken and Sue Kramer were directors, actors and administrators — not playwrights. Continually and mercilessly stretching themselves to the limits of their physical resources, neither had the time, talent or inclination to write new plays.

Cynics might remark that a theatre style as minimal as that developed by Brian Way succeeded more for economic than artistic or philosophical reasons. It is true that a script written for five actors to perform on a flat floor, with minimal props and costumes in available light, is less expensive to produce than any other scripts available up to that time. Although the Brian Way participation plays enjoyed a brief vogue in the mid-sixties and inspired innumerable imitations by writers of various expertise and understanding of the principles involved, few companies stayed with the style for long.[5] Globe, however, did. And they were successful. A summary of statistics for the first three seasons appears in Globe Theatre's Annual Report for 1968/69 as follows:

	1966-67	1967-68	1968-69
Number of weeks toured:	21½	20½	21½
Number of performances:	146	170	179
Number of students:	40,000	47,000	49,740
Number of miles:	15,000	13,500	17,839
Number of communities:	66	66	79

By the fifth season, 61,553 school children saw the plays and at the end of the ninth season, the Annual Report notes that with over 75,000 students and 20,000 adults in attendance at their performances, over ten percent of the province had been serviced.

Many professional theatres in Canada, which began as companies performing exclusively for young people, added

105

A discussion between actors and audience follows a production of a Globe Theatre children's play, which is usually performed in the school gymnasium

adult seasons or combined with adult professional theatres. When the child is parent of the adult, what happens to the child? It sometimes suffers a loss of identity; it almost invariably makes diminished demands on resources. Adult theatre is more risky, more expensive and more subject to professional criticism. The captive audience of the school tour has few counterparts in adult theatre. It is tempting to take theatre for young audiences for granted and to divert energy toward the more difficult task of attracting a large paying public to the adult season. At Globe Theatre, the addition of programming for adults was gradual.

The opportunity to present a play in eight Saskatchewan communities as a part of the 1968 Annual Festival of the Arts sponsored by the Saskatchewan Arts Board, led to the preparation and production of Bertolt Brecht's *The Good Woman of Setzuan* directed by Kenneth Kramer and starring Sue Richmond (Kramer) in the title role. Through personal initiative, sponsors were found for thirty more performances, many in towns of less than 1,000 population. Audience response was enthusiastic.

The Good Woman of Setzuan is ambitious programming; Brecht appears infrequently on the seasons of Canada's regional theatres. To choose it for their first offering for adults showed several things about the Kramers and the Globe. One was their faith in their audience's ability to accept challenging and thoughtful plays, another was a continuing interest in the theatre as a platform for social and political change. Although the adult season at Globe in recent years has included such popular hits as *You're a Good Man Charlie Brown* and *How the Other Half Loves,* the emphasis in most seasons has been upon plays like Wesker's *Roots,* Shaw's *Major Barbara,* Peterson's *The Great Hunger,* Ryga's *The Ecstasy of Rita Joe* and Langley's *Bethune.* This concern for community relevance and social conscience did not touch the Globe's schools program as obviously for some time. The first effect of the adult season on the schools tours was administrative:

> A major organizational experiment was carried
> out in the fall to make maximum use of the ten
> actors engaged for the tour (the eleventh was
> Sue Kramer, who played only in the adult pro-
> gram.) The ten actors were all used in *The
> Good Woman.* Four of them were used to make
> up the company playing the elementary
> program, and the remaining six were used to
> make up the company playing the secondary
> program. During the day, each of the smaller
> companies did one performance in the schools
> and then the two companies came together in
> the evening to play *The Good Woman.* During
> weeks when *The Good Woman* was not played,
> the two companies separated to different parts of
> the province to do two school performances per
> day.[6]

It is generally agreed among those concerned with theatre for young people that it is healthier, artistically, to perform in a company which includes both adult and family performances. In this regard, Globe Theatre's fall tour moved toward an ideal which, if maintained, could not help but attract more mature and experienced actors to the company. The spring tour *3 X 3* — a program of one-act plays: John Morton's *Box and Cox,* William Saroyan's *Hello, Out There* and Chekhov's *The Marriage Proposal,* adapted by Ken

Kramer to a Saskatchewan milieu — consolidated the repertory principle. Unfortunately, subsequent developments in establishing an adult repertory company for Regina and the attempt to continue the adult tours, resulted in economic strains which eventually made two separate companies a necessity.

In 1969, Frances Hyland starred in Aleksandr Volodin's *Five Evenings* for Globe's adult season. That the school performances suffered from demands of the adult plays that year, at least in some respects, is noted in a press release from Globe in December, 1969. "The adult production was more elaborate than last year and for this reason Globe was not able to play as many school bookings as usual on the fall tour." This is one instance, among many, where the schools tours were accommodated after the needs of the adult season were served.

Two separate companies, performing simultaneously under the Globe banner occurred for the first time in 1970, when plays presented free at the Regina Public Library were "sellouts" and helped justify the establishment of a permanent adult repertory company in Regina. The opportunity to use space in the new Saskatchewan Centre of the Arts for an expanded adult season seemed an auspicious omen:

At this juncture the directors look upon the
1970-71 season with an excitement and fear un-
matched since the first season of 1966-67. The
pressures for expansion can no longer be re-
sisted. The opening of the Saskatchewan
Centre of the Arts, with its ideally sized (for us)
Jubilee Theatre, plus a continued demand for
more adult programming has prompted us to
expand into two full companies: Globe I,
serving the schools in the province, and Globe
II, serving our growing adult audience.

Artistically, this is precisely the right time to
make this expansion: our audiences have
grown organically to such an extent that we can
no longer serve them with one company; hence,
our excitement. Economically, it is the wrong
moment with Saskatchewan going through its
worst economic crisis years; hence, our fears.[7]

The 1970-71 season was a difficult one for the company. Plans were, perhaps, too ambitious. The attempt to mount six plays in Regina, to continue the adult touring company and to maintain the schools company taxed both physical and financial resources. Equity requirements for the expanded company included the hiring of a professional stage manager. Personality clashes developed and relations between the Arts Centre and Globe administrations and the stage manager deteriorated under increased pressures in the second half of the season.

Ken Kramer had, not surprisingly, opted to work primarily in Regina, to establish the new adult company. To direct the schools tours, James Brewer was hired from London. An experienced actor, writer, stage manager and director, with extensive experience in all aspects of Brian Way's work at the Theatre Centre, Brewer was an excellent choice for a company whose faith in participation plays and in Brian Way's scripts had never wavered. All but one of the school shows of the 1971-72 season were directed by James Brewer and for the sixth straight season attendance increased. It was obvious that these plays satisfied Saskatchewan schools.

One of the positive aspects of the first, near-disastrous year in the Arts Centre had been the immense popularity of the original documentary drama, *Next Year Country*,[8] by Carol Bolt. Globe Theatre's personnel has often included couples: Paddy Campbell and Douglas Riske, Ann and Gary Stephens, Susan and Michael Hogan, Margaret and Bartley Bard—all worked for Globe in its first five seasons. But the couples who were to make the most lasting impact on the company's future were David and Carol Bolt (actor and playwright) and Rex and Rita Deverell (playwright and actress.) *Next Year Country*, marked an important "first" for Globe Theatre because its success encouraged it to embark upon increasingly ambitious schemes to commission and perform new works. Also, *Next Year Country*, although for adults, grew organically out of the circumstances of school tours. Carol Bolt drew upon her meetings with the people of Saskatchewan from times when she had accompanied her husband David on tour.

Two years later, for the 1972-73 season, Rex Deverell began his polemic prairie plays for young people. The inspiration for the content and characters had come for him, too, from observations of Globe School tours in which his wife Rita performed. With his *Shortshrift*, Globe's work for young people began to reflect more accurately the directors' avowed goals of creating an indigenous context and relevance. In the play, inhabitants of a small prairie town have been stricken by a strange malady: they have lost all *joie de vivre*. Fred, one of the town's fourteen inhabitants, goes to Grand City to the government buildings to try to discover what's wrong. He suspects that the disappearance of the town's sign, *"Shortshrift—we may not be big but we're happy,"* is connected with the despair. His encounter with government illustrates dramatically the remoteness of bureaucracy, the individual's frustration in dealing with an unresponsive system and, eventually, the triumph of caring and co-operation:

FRED: *turning his attention to the government building*
That's the biggest building I have ever seen in my whole life. *Puzzled.* That's funny. There's nobody around. Not a soul. I would have thought the place would have been a beehive buzzing with activity, you know — being the government and all. But nobody is around. Well, I'll just go up these steps and knock on these huge doors. *He mounts the steps and is about to knock on the doors when the door opens automatically.* They're opening! Must have seen me coming. Hello, yoohoo! That's odd. Whoever opened the doors has completely vanished. Look in here. This great hallway and not a person here.

VOICE: Welcome to the government. This
            is a recording. Please state
            your name and purpose at the
            sound of the tone. Thank you.

FRED: *looking around*
            Where are you?

VOICE: You have five seconds.
            There is an electronic beep.

FRED: *startled*   My-name-is-Fred-and-
            my-purpose-for-being-here-is-
            to-find-out-what's-happening-
            to-Shortshrift.   *There is
            another electronic beep.*

VOICE: Thank you very much. Please
            take a seat and wait until fur-
            ther notice.

FRED: Darndest fool thing I ever
            heard of.

VOICE B: Thank you for waiting.   *Fred
            stands up.*   Please wait a
            little longer.

FRED: Hey! Just a minute. . . .

VOICE B: This is a recording.

FRED: Oh.   *Fred sits down.*

VOICE C: Thank you for waiting.   *Pause.*
            Are you still there?

FRED: *surprised*   I thought you
            were a recording.

VOICE C: This is a recording. Please leave your telephone number at the sound of the tone. One of our people will telephone you within the next month. Thank you for calling upon your government. If we may be of service in the future, we hope you will call on us again. Office hours are nine to five, Monday through Friday.

FRED: *his voice overlapping the recording* Now just one minute. I haven't got next month. I've only got today. And this thing is important, you hear?

VOICE C: Your telephone number please. *Beep.*

FRED: I'm not going to leave any number. I want to talk to a live human being, right now, you hear? No, you can't hear, you dumb machine. . . . *Two beeps.*

VOICE C: I'm sorry. There is no telephone listing of that nature. Would you please repeat it more clearly. *Beep.*

FRED: I'm sorry too. I'm not leaving here until I get to talk to somebody! *Beep.*

VOICE: I'm sorry sir. . . .

FRED:	I'm sorry! I'm sorry! Is that all you can say? "I'm sorry."
VOICES:	I'm sorry. *Beep.* I'm sorry. *Beep.*

> *A door opens and Quack
> rushes out.* [11]

The sharp sense of comic timing combined with the sincere sympathy the audience had built up for Fred and our common experience of frustration with inhuman elements of bureaucracy make this scene an example of Rex Deverell at his best. We care about Fred and what happens to him.

Unfortunately, in some Deverell scripts characterization rests almost entirely with the name — Toofine, Typhoon, Shivers and Quack are exactly what each name implies, leaving little for an actors invention. To be fair, many features of this form were dictated by necessity, not planned as policy. One must play "between two bells," or for about forty-five minutes. Four actors are often all that the budget allows. The space is almost always the school's gymnasium, where an aesthetic scene design is almost impossible. No stage lighting is used. eliminating yet another tool for theatricality. In Canada's school tours the pay is low, tour conditions are gruelling and prestige is non-existent. Some actors have enjoyed the work with young people enough to tour for two, possibly three seasons, but those who would think of touring in the schools as a lifetime career must be extremely rare. Globe has only had occasional repeaters on the tours and Ken Kramer has bemoaned the fact that much of his time each new season is spent in teaching the newly assembled cast fundamental attitudes and techniques, leaving less time for rehearsal of the actual scripts. If a company were to work together even for five years, they would know each other and about touring. They would know about playing for young people and could proceed with confidence to the tasks at hand.

Actors should have the opportunity to play roles from the classic repertoire and in challenging new works. Globe's first regular season combined the casts of the Regina company,

A Globe Theatre actress receives some helpful advice from one of her audience on tour

the adult touring company and the school tours in a production of Shaw's *Saint Joan*. For two successive seasons, a
Christmas show attempted to combine the actors of both companies for performances in Globe's new home.

The acquisition of a permanent space of its own marked a
significant milestone in the growth of Globe Theatre.
Globe performed in the Saskatchewan Arts Centre for three
years. Although subscriptions and attendance increased each
year, the founding directors realized that a home of their own
was essential. For one thing, the atmosphere of the Arts Centre
was elitist. One had to worry about what to wear and trans-
portation for people without private cars. For the Kramers,
who believed that theatre should be accessible and cheap
these problems loomed large. It was difficult to exercise complete control as tenants. An abandoned bank building in the
heart of downtown Regina became the permanent home of
Globe. George Ryga's *The Ecstasy of Rita Joe* opened as scheduled, on November 27, 1973, in a half-painted room, with no
carpet on the floor and the cast and the audience sharing the
second floor washrooms.

The intimate theatre-in-the-round created on the ground
floor of the building, seating 196 people on tiered padded
benches, is utilitarian but pleasant. The Kramers have never

made visual splendour a high priority. The preference for theatre-in-the-round seems to be both philosophical and pragmatic. The plays for children by Brian Way took their shape from Way's observation of boys and girls: intimacy was important. Also, the theatre, style and repertoire of Peter Cheeseman at Stoke-on-Trent in England had been an inspiration to the Kramers, as powerful as that of Brian Way. Pragmatically, it was the kind of theatre that people in Saskatchewan were willing to support. Globe has always been fiscally responsible. Rarely has it been in debt. Alberta Theatre Projects, where scenic design and lighting have always been important, had a six-figure deficit in 1975*; Globe's was $664.00. Although other factors enter into the reasons for this discrepancy, the main difference lies in the style of presentation of the two companies.

There are a lot of solid achievements to look back on and several honours earned. Globe's schools program, *Shakespeare's Women*, was one of three English-language productions chosen by adjudicator Donald Wetmore to represent Canada at the Fourth General Assembly of ASSITEJ in Montréal in 1972. The National Film Board used Globe actors and directorial assistance for its half-hour documentary, *Tales from a Prairie Drifter*, based on Rod Langley's play, produced by Globe in its 1972-73 season. Globe won the prestigious Ohio Award for distinction in television programming twice — once for "Sue's Place," an integrated arts education show devised by Ken and performed by Sue Kramer, and for *Julius Caesar*, an episoide in a series called "Shakespeare and The Globe," which featured participation by a large group of high school students, along with Globe actors. And in 1976, Globe went to Montréal to represent Saskatchewan at the cultural events of the Olympics. They chose to take three of Rex Deverell's prairie plays, written for the school tours. *Shortshrift, The Copetown City Kite Crisis* and *The Shinbone General Store Caper* were revised and appeared under the omnibus title: *Next Town Nine Miles*.

During their tenth anniversary season the Kramers invited Brian Way to Saskatchewan to direct *Hamlet*. The production,

---

*ATP has wiped out its debt in the past three seasons, mainly by increasing ticket sales but without sacrificing its excellent production values. (*J.D.*)

starring the Kramers in the roles of Hamlet and Gertrude aptly celebrated the links between The Theatre Centre and the Globe, Shakespeare and the Globe, Brian Way and the (new) Globe. It was to commemorate the end of an era.

In retrospect, it seems a particularly fortuitous fate which led the Kramers to Regina. Their belief that theatre should be socially active and their efforts to keep it from becoming elitist, either in price or repertoire, fit into the political and social climate of Saskatchewan, with its long tradition of agrarian reform and populist policies. Their determination, personal stamina and wide range of combined talents and capabilities undoubtedly account for the survival of the company in its first, difficult years. Paradoxically, it is one of those early "pluses" which later hindered the quality of the company's work. To direct, design, administrate and act within one company of five is an understandable, even admirable economy. To continue to play "all parts" in an elaborate operation with a six-figure budget seems vainglorious or self-defeating to some observers.

Sue Kramer has said that in many ways Globe is "stuck in a very traditional pattern—which isn't necessarily the *right* pattern." It was a method they evolved when they started the company and it has enabled them to survive, but Sue thinks that "maybe we need to dig and experiment." The 1975-76 season showed some of this idealism in action. The appointment of Rex Deverell in residence as a playwright for young people was a first in Canada. He has been re-appointed in subsequent seasons. His first full-length play for adult audiences, *Boiler Room Suite,* was premiered at Globe in 1977.

If the modest design elements in Globe's school productions were assigned a slightly higher priority than in the past, with the employment of a designer of more than ordinary imagination and expertise, the visual impact of the performances upon young audiences would be greatly enhanced. And if ways and means could be found to employ actors for several seasons, the level of performance in the school tours might match more closely the quality of the scripts.

Since 1966 Globe Theatre has enjoyed the same artistic direction, practised responsible fiscal policies and encouraged innovation through the commissioning of new plays for both adults and children. Ken and Sue Kramer have created a company which became a prototype for many others in Canada. Their discovery and encouragement in Rex Deverell of a playwright who combines participation plays in schools with regional content has made an exceptional contribution to Canadian theatre.

Footnotes

1. Maynard, Fredelle Bruser. *Raisins and Almonds,* Paperjacks, Don Mills, 1975, p. 187.
2. Kramer, Ken. Audiotape, February, 1975.
3. Kramer, Sue. Audiotape, February, 1975.
4. Kramer, Ken, *op. cit.*
5. YOUTHEATRE in Montreal is one outstanding exception to this general observation.
6. Globe Theatre Annual Report, 1968-69, p. 4.
7. "The Future," Globe Theatre Annual Report, 1969-70.
8. Rewritten and later published as *Buffalo Jump* in *Carol Bolt: Playwright in Profile,* Playwright's Co-op, Toronto, 1976.
9. Deverell, Rex. Audiotape, Interview with Elaine Waese, Regina, Saskatchewan, August, 1975, CBC/Toronto.
10. Deverell, Rex, *op. cit.*
11. Deverell, Rex. *Shortshrift,* Playwright's Co-op, Toronto, 1972, pp. 14-15.

117

Evolving Our Own Ways—Colonial, Native and Pioneer

The directors of both the Alberta Theatre Projects and the Mermaid Theatre evolved their repertoire from importing plays to producing native legends and Canadian works about the early pioneer period. Douglas Riske began staging plays for young audiences with the Allied Arts Centre Company in Calgary. Two of the first scripts were Brian Way's *The Bell* and Paddy Campbell's *In the Enchanted Box*. Campbell's first play was modelled on Way's participation plays. She herself admits that it was derivative and that the language sounded British, not Canadian. Riske also included the classics in the Allied Arts Centre tour of junior and senior high schools.

The same colonial phase is found in Mermaid's beginnings. But Way's plays were a failure in Nova Scotia; they proved foreign to children in the Maritimes. At first, adaptations of fables and classics also filled out Mermaid repertoire. Laying the groundwork for a company involves a search for identity, status and security. It seems that successful scripts, albeit foreign, are a place to start. The other factor was the scarcity of the right kind of Canadian material in the 1960's and early 1970's. Both companies soon found, however, that there was a richness to be found at home. It was not a rejection of international scripts, but a need to delve deeply into national identity that turned their focus to Canada's native legends and early history. Both companies are to be commended for their insight and courage in this pioneer work.

The native peoples of Canada are demanding that notice be taken of their cultural as well as aboriginal rights. With this new awareness has come the strong conviction that it be reflected in Canada's arts. One of the first effects has been negative. It is no longer considered appropriate for a non-native person to portray in art, music, drama or dance the culture of the native peoples. Folklore has formed generally a significant segment of any nation's repertoire of theatre for young audiences. The diverse arts and rich heritage of native Indians of the Inuit has been, not surprisingly, the subject of many Canadian plays for young people. On the whole, one is impressed with the care with which writers have approached this material. Henry Beissel's *Inook and the Sun* has been performed in many countries. He is careful in his introduction to the play to explain that:

> *Inook* is an Eskimo play only in the sense that its
> characters, its place, and its imagery are
> Eskimo. The story and its perspectives are
> mine, and I have no idea if an Eskimo will
> recognize himself and his world in the play. Nor
> do I think that it matters. Years ago I studied
> Eskimo life and culture, and what I
> encountered there never lost its hold over my
> imagination. In the Arctic, I found
> fundamental patterns of life and death and
> quest lying open to the mind that are buried
> in our urban civilization. The stark realities of
> the conflict between summer and winter, light
> and dark, heat and cold, and the struggle to
> survive between them, seemed to call out for
> dramatic treatment, though it was some time
> before the shape of the play emerged.[1]

Beissel goes on to explain that the form was inspired by the
Bunraku puppet plays of Japan; he feels no similar urge to
apologize for borrowing from the Orient.

Len Peterson's *Almighty Voice* tells the poignant story of a
tragic rebellion by one Indian against the white man's code. In
a sensitive essay, "On the Trail of Almighty Voice," Peterson
explains his own feelings about the links in Canada between
Whiteskins and Indians:

> The longer we went to school, and the more we
> learned of great men and great happenings
> elsewhere, the less regard we had for ourselves.
> We were nobodies.
>
> Yet at play we didn't feel like that. Running,
> wrestling, sunning ourselves, swimming,
> skating, tumbling, throwing foot-, base-, and
> snowballs, and contending in marksmanship,
> strength and clowning in our big sky world, we
> were solid, noisy somebodies.

We felt substantial, too, astride a horse,
swinging a hammer, digging potatoes, stooking
and splitting wood. "Noticeable on the
horizon," the sodbusters said.[2]

It is this essence of boyhood and the love of the land and the
horse which makes Bonnie LeMay's play for Alberta Theatre
Projects, *Boy Who Has a Horse,* so moving in production and
so gripping to the young audiences who watched the young
hero sacrifice a symbol and extension of his selfhood, his horse,
to the larger cause of survival of the tribe.

With Len Peterson, it is not only a shared experience of
games and play that forms a bond between Indian and
Whiteskin. More importantly it is:

Geography. We shared the same geography as
the Indians. We kids figured that out on our
own. We behaved the same in a blizzard as
Indian kids. No division there. Water to drink,
water to swim in, and frozen water to slide on
were as wondrous to us as them.[3]

It was over different ideas of ownership of the land that the
battles between Whiteskins and Indians developed. In Len
Peterson's view, geography always wins, but it is a long process.
In the timelessness which begins all history, Peterson believes
that the accumulation of wisdom of the Indians will be at least
as important as the "truths" of the civilization which devoured
it:

We begin there. At one with our Indian past.
Embracing our Indian present and presence,
and making amends for our trickery and
injustices. At one with our alien nomads from
overseas. Building on that maybe, we will cease
floundering, fretting and warring in our
geography and history and flourish in them.

Was there not some vision of that in Almighty
Voice's defiance and agony?

The play, *Almighty Voice,* is part of my back-
tracking. It's for young people, but adults may
watch.

On the Trail of Almighty Voice is more back-
tracking. It's for adults. But young people may
read.[4]

Often an Indian is used by the playwright as a symbol of
social injustice. Carol Bolt's musical, *Cyclone Jack,* is in some
ways a history play, but its message is one of social injustice.
We see Tom Longboat's love of running exploited: as long as
Tom wins races, he's a hero; when he loses, he becomes the
driver of a garbage truck. Native lore and history appear in
several of Paddy Campbell's plays and the changes in emphasis
reflect her growth as well as the changes in attitudes by and
about native peoples in the past ten years. *Chinook,* the second
play written by Paddy Campbell for the Arts Centre Company
of Calgary, is based on an Indian legend to explain the
phenomenon of the warm winter wind which sweeps through
the mountain passes of the Rockies, melting snow and ice
within minutes. It is a participation play for a very young
audience. Its lack of pretension, opportunities for dance
drama and engaging characters have made it very popular
since it was first performed. But when she wrote *The History
Show* and later, *Under the Arch,* the Indian's treatment by
white men was at once more satirical and serious. Indian
religion was portrayed with dignity and used as the reality
against the music hall turns. And in *Madwitch,* written for
elementary school children, the old woman who happens to be
Indian, is used as a symbol of unthinking prejudice. George
Ryga's *The Ecstasy of Rita Joe* has become a staple of
Canadian content in the high school curriculum. Performed in
most regional theatres and toured worldwide in the Royal
Winnipeg Ballet's dance version, it is probably the best-known
view of the Canadian Indian.

Mermaid's epic plays based on the Micmac Indian legends
are the main focus of the company. This is being
supplemented by material from the pioneer period. The
subject is also popular in many of Alberta Theatre Projects
productions. One notable script, *The Judgement of Clifford*

Sifton, relates many touching hardships that pioneer men, women and children had to endure in order to populate the "last best west." An intimate perspective on pioneering is given in *Susanna Moodie* by Mermaid Theatre, in which an intelligent, sensitive woman tells of her fears and tortures:

My brain gropes nervous
tentacles in the night, sends out
fears hairy as bears,
demands lamps; or waiting

for my shadowy husband, hears
malice in the trees' whispers.[5]

Alberta Theatre Projects has also produced many memorable plays about the early days of the Canadian West, including the stark and parched prairie tale, *The Day Jake Made Her Rain,* by W.O. Mitchell.

While the bulk of Mermaid's themes are native and most of ATP's are about pioneers, both have produced a large amount of original, commissioned scripts by regional authors. These companies are deeply rooted in a geographical environment and are committed to the indigenous culture of their region.

Footnotes

1. Beissel, Henry. *Inook and the Sun,* Playwright's Co-op, 1974, p. 7.
2. Peterson, Leonard. *Almighty Voice,* Book Society of Canada, Agincourt, 1974, p. viii.
3. *Ibid.,* p. ix.
4. *Ibid.,* pp. xiv-xv.
5. Smyth, Donna E. *Susanna Moodie,* An Unpublished Script Produced by Mermaid Theatre, Wolfville, Nova Scotia.

Masks, Myths and a Vision: Mermaid Theatre
of Wolfville, Nova Scotia

In the shadow of North Mountain and Cape Blomidon, Glooscap, the legendary hero of the Micmac Indians oversees the lush Annapolis Valley and Wolfville, Nova Scotia. On Main Street, Wolfville (population 2,831), an older three-gabled house with a large double garage in the backyard houses a dozen artists rehearsing. Mermaid: the word conjures up images of fanciful sea creatures, fairy tales, or London theatre. There is something of that, and more, in the heredity of Mermaid Theatre Company, which has gained national and international recognition.

Apart from the out-of-province tours and urban performances, Mermaid is committed to bringing professional theatre to Maritime rural communities where it is seldom or never seen. Mermaid also has an intense commitment to writing about Nova Scotia's heritage, both native and pioneer, by local playwrights and performed by Maritime actors.

The three directors—Evelyn Garbary, Tom Miller and Lee Lewis—share the same vision for Mermaid. The division of labour is capped with mutual respect for each others' talents. Artistic decisions are made jointly by Garbary and Miller with openness. Evelyn Garbary's writing is often spiced and interwoven with suggestions from Tom Miller. The triumvirate is realistic, willing to work within social restrictions, yet nurturing a vision which is the central force in all their lives.

Dedication to indigenous culture is not new to Evelyn Garbary, founder and director of Mermaid. She will occasionally allude to her rich experiences in the theatre. An early childhood in Wales has left her with a love of the countryside and its inhabitants. Diverse forces moulded her adolescence: reading Shakespeare, dance lessons in the style of Isadora Duncan and elocution lessons in boarding school. There followed a Gold Medal at the London Academy of Music and Dramatic Arts, apprenticeship at the Old Vic, and touring with an English repertory company. This training was invaluable in teaching her discipline and professionalism from such people as John Gielgud, William Poel and Harley Granville-Barker. She also experienced the rigours of touring ten shows in nine months, followed by a Canadian tour.

At twenty-one, she had a vision of a Welsh National Theatre Company producing bilingual plays. Returning to her homeland, Garbary started the first experimental Welsh theatre with the same ideal as W.B. Yeats who championed the Irish dramatic movement. "One must get in touch with one's cultural roots to express life; not to search for a style but to dramatize the folk imagination."

She moved to London, married, and soon longed to be in theatre again. Her social life reads like a who's who, including W.B. Yeats and Evelyn Waugh. Later, the Abbey Players and the Gate Theatre in Dublin introduced her to different acting styles. Cyril Cusack and Shelah Richards, among other colleagues, used the Stanislavsky and Antoine techniques of building a character.

Emigrating to Canada in 1956, she left Toronto quickly in search of a rural setting. Mrs. Garbary has consciously avoided "colonizing"; her approach has been to listen to what Canadians are saying. In 1971, she heard students at Acadia University talking about "help, children and theatre." From such needs and the benevolence of federal grants, emerged a theatre company:

> I never thought of theatre for the young as
> being my thing at all. One of my closest friends
> had been in child drama but we used to avoid
> talking about it because at that time it never
> made sense to me. It used to upset me. Now I've
> had to think about it, I know what it's about
> and I can talk to her.[1]

Evelyn Garbary has thrown the word "children" out of Mermaid's terms of reference because it is too condescending. She prefers to give young audiences too much, as in *The Invisible Hunter,* rather than challenge them too little as some plays for children do.

Her emergence as principal playwright for Mermaid happened quite by accident:

> I had been writing for CBC, Radio Erin and
> BBC, but didn't start writing for Mermaid until
> one night the three of us were sitting here about

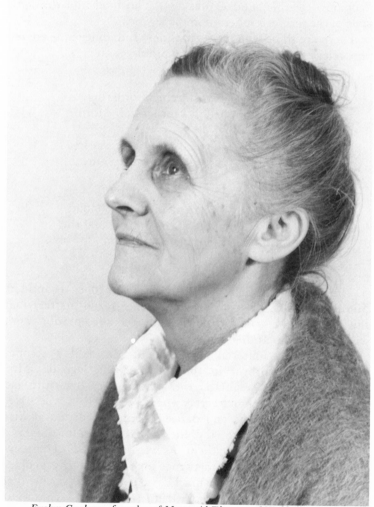

Evelyn Garbary, founder of Mermaid Theatre of Wolfville, Nova Scotia

10 p.m. The script in rehearsal was not
working, the company could not come to terms
with it. So I said, "Get out." I started writing
and I haven't stopped since.[2]

She had come across the Micmac legends and immediately
realized that this was the right material.[3] Silas Rand, a
minister who learned the Micmac language described it as
"copious, flexible, and expressive." The bold and dramatic
style of the scripts is inherent in the legends.

There are some who think that these Indian legends are not
very relevant. Some of the cultural problems are:

1.) The difference in hierarchical ordering: is
the god or hero defined in a recognizable form?

2.) The legends interweave various stories:
should the author pattern them neatly into a
beginning, middle and an end?

3.) The contradictory nature of the good/bad
Indian hero: will the audience comprehend the
struggle within the different social system?

The arguments seem to break down if one reconsiders
Mermaid's objective to present good theatre no matter what
the source. The crucial issue is: does the presentation work
with a particular audience?

The Micmac material also brought Mermaid a responsibility to be faithful to the spirit of the legends. Mrs.
Garbary consulted regularly with Micmac teachers to make
sure that traditional characters where presented in true style,
with the proper music and dance. Mermaid worried at first
about bringing the material to the Indian people, for there is a
growing militancy among them. As it turned out, the company
has won a great deal of acceptance among the native people.
In 1975, two men (nineteen and twenty-three years of age)
were financed by the Department of Indian Affairs to
apprentice with Mermaid. The trainees were to learn about the

Evelyn Garbary, Lee Lewis and Tom Miller, co-directors of Mermaid
Theatre of Wolfville, Nova Scotia

art of theatre and the production of Micmac stories in particular. Having had little or no experience with the many demands of production and touring, the apprenticeships proved difficult. Eventually, it was decided that a better procedure would be for Mermaid to make itself available at the specific request of the Micmac people. During Mermaid tours, Indian children saw for the first time their own people on stage and theatre as a valid profession.

Enter Tom Miller with an interdisciplinary background in the arts. As a Baptist minister's son, church activities had given him opportunities to communicate and work with others. Having studied and instructed in basic design and drawing, Miller emigrated to Canada in 1970 as an Art Consultant to the Kings County Amalgamated School Board of Nova Scotia. It was in this job that he searched for a stimulating experience to give to school children in the visual arts. He remembered a marionette company and the excitement it generated in his school days. Puppets, masks and theatre soon became his life's focus. Mermaid provided him with the outlet.

129

As a designer, Miller claims not to adhere to any rigid theory, but rather to choose "what works":

> Visual ideas come from various sources to
> interpret the moment in the play and fulfill
> some technical uses as well. We had needs and
> we responded to them: *e.g.*, the gods in the
> legends needed height and we gave them height
> as giant puppet-actors in order to solve that
> problem.[4]

The combination of masks, puppets and actors opens up imaginative possibilities. Many children attest to their excitement and the vivid stage presentations remain in their memories.

Unquestionably, Miller's visual design is a powerful element in the Mermaid presentations. And the Mermaid has unified his skills into a harmony of music, words, design and improvisation which is live theatre.

A quiet dynamo of a woman, Lee Lewis markets the creative products of Mermaid to communities, school boards, impressarios and governments. A graduate of McGill University, she worked closely with a major impressario in her native Montréal, helped to found Les Feux Follets, a dance company, and to build Folkways Recordings, dedicated to developing Canadian artists. Upon joining Mermaid, she was given all the duties not directly related to stage production: finances, liaison, contracts, bookings, banking.

The three co-directors meet infrequently on specific issues. Decisions are made by consensus except that Mrs. Lewis does not involve herself with staging. During final rehearsals, she will observe and offer her comments as an audience member. Her artistic influence on Mermaid has been her strong commitment to Indian legends and the development of other Nova Scotian material.

Financial policy, a tricky job at the best of times, is to avoid deficit funding:

> We've chosen to look for a commercial sponsor
> rather than go into deficit funding which we
> refuse to do. We work night and day exploring

Mermaid Theatre on tour

opportunities. We want to work 12 months a
year, but we will not go into deficit funding.[5]

Given faith, common sense and the committed energies of
the directors, Mermaid manages to pay approximately twelve
people almost year round. One year, Miller toured on an
Equity minimum salary, his only income. Garbary earned
$1,000.00 in director's fees.

Low overheads ease Mermaid's financial burden. In the
past, Acadia University donated its premises. Then Mrs.
Garbary built and paid for an enormous "double garage" on
her property which serves as the rehearsal studio. Mermaid
could not afford to run the same operation in a large centre if
it had to rent facilities. Mermaid appears to be financially one
of the best managed theatres for young audiences in Canada.
All this success is not without its compromises, and the
directors are practical enough to accept these. Margaret-Ann
Cain, former stage manager for Mermaid, says that her
fondest wish for the profession would be to have funding
available so that one could achieve the same technical
standards as adult theatre and get away from the constant

compromises "which are the name of the game" in theatre for young people.

The company takes time to rehearse, then leaves the play for a couple of weeks or more so that the author can change the script. The actors then are recalled for more rehearsal. It is the ideal way of developing original scripts. According to Lee Lewis, the participation plays borrowed from England seemed foreign to the children of Nova Scotia. The rural audiences were reserved in their responses and the plays did not seem to speak intimately to them. Mermaid states that it prefers now to play family shows to a variety of age groups. Another reason for having moved away from participation plays was the restriction on audience size. Large numbers reduce the spontaneity and intent of the shows.

Mermaid's first season included an imported Brian Way play, several adaptations of classics and some original scripts. The following year, *The Micmac Legends* by Elizabeth Jones was the most popular part of the repertoire which included *Fables and Folktales, The Merchant of Venice,* and *Evangeline.* The third season, *Glooscap's People,* adapted by Evelyn Garbary from a script by Elizabeth Jones, was given the most performances. It was translated into French as *Le Monde de Glooscap* and another Micmac legend, *The Journey,* by Evelyn Garbary was added to the repertoire. In these Indian themes, Mermaid offers an epic vision of life, non-realistic images that speak to the subconscious. Heroes are reminiscent of the ancient Greek world where men and gods are matched. The epic is a natural form for adapting legends for the contemporary stage:

> One of the interesting things in the Mermaid epic
> scripts is the coming to terms with courage,
> risk, challenge, failure, success, the uncertainty
> of the reality and finding powers within oneself
> and in the cosmos to draw upon to deal with
> these.

> This can be pointed out and metaphorically
> sensed, but it cannot be taught. In the Eskimo
> and Indian cultures, they have heroes who are
> archetypal models of achievement for coping,

Lionel Simmons

The Brothers *was written and directed by Evelyn Garbary and designed by Tom Miller*

for the way one organizes energies for living.
Contemporary culture heroes are celebrities,
not models for virtue and fulfillment.[6]

Although Mrs. Garbary is the principal writer, others have written for Mermaid, including Elizabeth Jones and Donna E. Smyth. Commissioning scripts has its own problems. Mrs. Garbary has experienced the geographical and symbolic distances between authors and companies. It is costly to engage well-known authors for the length of time it takes to become acquainted with the company's style, write a play, and then follow it through rehearsal and rewriting. The proximity of authors has been a necessity, not just a convenience.

Mermaid also makes specific demands on actors. Some of its most adept actors came with a non-theatrical background. Previous exposure to training sometimes "ruins" the actor for the company's performance style. Many of Mermaid's most successful actors have been teachers who understand and relate to young people. Rather than auditioning in large centres for experienced actors, first consideration is given to Maritime actors as a matter of policy. The directors feel that local actors understand better the audiences and seem to know how to relate to them in schools and community halls. Actors often lack training or interest in mask, mime or puppetry as demanded by the company. In *Glooscap and the Mighty Bullfrog*, fifteen roles are played by eight actors. One actor may dance, mime and perform in mask — all in one play. Mermaid demands versatility in interest, talent and technique.

Mrs. Garbary believes strongly that acting is an intuitive process. She likens acting to being in a trance, an outside force taking over while the actor's ego loses itself in the character. Her views relate to Keith Johnstone's approach to acting:

> I see a direct connection between mask, or pos-
> sessed state, and that of the deeply concen-
> trated actor. . . .[7]

Johnstone and Garbary use different methods in rehearsal even though they appear to have similar expectations from actors. She may begin a rehearsal with blocking; he might use exercises to revitalize the actor's intuitive process. Garbary talks about the actor's problem in terms of "ego," whereas Johnstone states that it is merely self-censorship. This censorship produces an actor who "thinks" but does not know how to "be."

Mermaid faces the usual challenges in trying to build up a strong company of professional actors. The personal and professional need to grow is very strong in young actors. One told of the crises he went through, his need for recognition among peers and for intelligent reviews. It took him three years to accept playing for young audiences as a legitimate profession. Mrs. Garbary approached some mature actors to play in *Susanna Moodie* and the response was distant: "Do you expect me to do crew duty? I've been through that." Even though it is hard to develop actors in Mermaid's style because of the constant turnover (the eternal search for the greener grass), the directors keep in mind the needs of each actor. The *Merchant of Venice* and *Dr. Faustus* were specifically chosen

Susanna Moodie *by Donna E. Smyth; designed by Tom Miller. Actress Mary Lou Rockwell has been with Mermaid Theatre since its inception.*

to challenge actors with classic material that required depth in understanding and technical skills. Actors are cast as much to stretch them as to use proven talents. In retrospect, many young actors may realize what range of experience they obtained.

Mermaid prefers mixed age groups not only in its actors, but also in its audiences. In schools, that is a change from most touring companies who insist on specialized age groups. Among native people there is no segregation by age for story-telling. It is an accepted fact that children's listening vocabulary is far above their reading one.

Some of the scripts in repertoire, however, cannot play to a school audience of only younger people. Mermaid feels that there could be disturbing elements in a play if there was no one to explain or listen to the child's question. It has nothing to do with being "too intellectual," but rather being careful to create the right conditions.

Mermaid plans a season around three age groups: primary to grade six, junior high and senior high/adult. The school imposes this chronological breakdown. Junior high tends to be the most demanding age group. Audience reactions change according to age, sophistication and exposure to previous theatre groups. Having played in Québec, Mermaid found that:

> French speaking audiences are more
> sophisticated in theatre experience. In Québec
> the working class young have a different
> cultural exposure. French-language television
> offers a more qualitative variety of comedy,
> monologue and political satire. They watch
> and listen differently.[8]

Part of the task in raising the standard of scripts is to educate teachers to treat challengingly material in a positive way. Often teachers claim that a certain play is "too hard" or "beyond their vocabulary level" or "too serious."

The assumption is that children should come to the theatre for entertainment, enjoyment and total comprehension. As long as these attitudes exist in educators, Mermaid will have to continue to produce different scripts for different age groups. Provided that the challenge to comprehension is not deeply disturbing, the child should be stretched intellectually, emotionally and socially by a theatre experience. Enjoyment is only part of the desired response to a play. Mermaid's plays:

> Put us into contact with the universal depths of
> human experience which have to be evoked and
> not taught. I think that there are significant
> realizations that can be evoked in a ten year old
> or six year old child. These must be told
> symbolically, not literally. And this is something
> human, it has nothing to do with being young.[9]

Dr. Herbert Lewis, a Philosophy Professor at Acadia, is unofficial critic, resource person and senior philosopher to Mermaid. He watches the final stages of rehearsal and offers his response. It happens in an informal manner. Mermaid also craves professional feedback to assist its growth. There has been little constructive criticism from colleagues in the theatre. In 1973, its second year of operation, the company played in Montréal. Myron Galloway reviewed the shows and other professionals gave their response. This was helpful and the company felt a sense of belonging to the larger artistic community. Not enough of this happens for young companies across Canada. The Montréal showcase is now remembered by Mermaid as a significant event, an impetus for self-analysis and growth.

The company from Wolfville has had glowing press coverage in many small and a few larger newspapers. The response from small communities tells Mermaid about the kind of impact it is having on the majority of its audience. *The Acadian Journal* says that Mermaid is the second professional theatre company in the province, but "the only professional Nova Scotian company if one considers the fact that The Neptune is notorious for out-of-province casting."

Some critics have disagreed with the strong visual element in Mermaid's presentation and fail to see full impact of the scripts. Vancouver critic, Max Wyman, called *The Invisible Hunter* a "Mickey Mouse treatment. . .lots of light and colour, but nothing to scare the kids." He further criticizes the whole show as "authenticity seen through a distorting mirror, and twisted truth is no truth at all."

There is a place in theatre for the retelling of ancient myths and legends. And ultimately this is the place for Mermaid. This is not to say that the scripts are without fault, but Mermaid is finding a polished and artistic style of its own. The company will achieve this only through writing, rehearsal and performance. To condemn Mermaid because it is imperfect is to forget its dreams and the limitations most small theatres are heir to.

Jo Anne Claus of *The Fredericton Gleaner* understood Mermaid's intent:

> They all approved it as splendid theatre. It was
> the stuff dreams (and nightmares) are made of.
> Good theatre should make us aware the world
> could topple about our ears at any moment.
> Every child left certain of that fact, and amazed
> (disturbed too) at having seen their private
> passions and violence openly dramatized as
> universal.[10]

During the summer of 1977, Mermaid also made a month-long tour, giving twenty-four performances in eight Welsh communities and four performances at the Royal Court Theatre in London. To have attended the Cumru 77 International Festival of Theatre for young people in Wales was a particular point of pride for Evelyn Garbary:

> The evening was a brilliant fusion of spectacle,
> dance, song and music and its rapturous
> reception is a fine tribute to Evelyn Garbary,
> the main writer and director, marking her
> return to her native Wales after nearly twenty
> years.[11]

Footnotes

1. Garbary, Evelyn. Audiotape, June, 1976.
2. *Ibid.*
3. a) Rand, Reverend Silas Tertius. *Legends of the Micmacs,* 1894.
   b) Leland, Charles G. *The Algonquin Legends of New England* or *Myths and Folklore of the Micmac, Passamaquoddy and Penobscot Tribes,* 1885.
4. Miller, Tom. Audiotape, June, 1976.
5. Lewis, Lee. Audiotape, June, 1976.
6. Lewis, Herbert. Audiotape, June, 1976.
7. Johnstone, Keith. "Acting" in *Discussions in Developmental Drama,* No. 4 University of Calgary, February, 1973, p. 6.
8. Lewis, Lee, *op cit.*
9. Lewis, Herbert, *op cit.*
10. Claus, Jo Anne. *The Daily Gleaner,* Fredericton, New Brunswick, May 22, 1975, p. 17.
11. Orchard, Rober. "Delightful Breath of Theatrical Fresh Air," *Western Mail,* Wales, July 15, 1977.

Through the Fields of Memory: Alberta Theatre Projects of Calgary

Climb on our wagon of Drama and Rhyme
Through the fields of memory
We'll chart a line through the mist of time
And relive a lost century.

Magic of the Music Hall
Blithely makes it all come to life
Laugh at human comedy
Share the misery of our strife.[1]

Alberta Theatre Projects was conceived as a production company presenting historical plays about Southern Alberta for school children brought to the Canmore Opera House in Heritage Park. This original goal has expanded over an eight year period to include new scripts for both adult and young audiences, plus other Canadian and non-Canadian material. The commitment to history and schools persists to the present. Both the adult subscription season and production of some non-Canadian scripts evolved in response to artistic as well as to community needs. ATP has played a significant role in enriching Alberta's cultural life and fostering several indigenous playwrights. This has endeared ATP to the Calgary community and helped the company to achieve national recognition.

The three founding members, Douglas Riske, Paddy Campbell and Lucille Wagner were concerned about a market for Canadian talent and appalled at the ignorance of Canadian history. The timely idea found support with the federal Local Initiatives Program. The company actually became a showcase project, the pride of LIP. By July, 1973, both the public and separate school boards of Calgary backed the theatre with funds. Some touring began in Southern Alberta, as well as performances in the Canmore Opera House.

ATP was the first theatre for young audiences to have its own home. The Canmore Opera House is an original log cabin structure inside Heritage Park. One of the company's stated goals is "to enable young people to experience live theatre in an historical setting." This has had its drawbacks: conversion costs, the long narrow shape of the house which holds only 165

Douglas Riske, Artistic Director of Alberta Theatre Projects of Calgary

The Canmore Opera House, home of Alberta Theatre Projects, is located in Calgary's Heritage Park

seats and the tiny (though ingeniously utilized) stage. Despite these limitations, a home was given ATP advantages over other touring companies for young audiences. It was easier to expand and include an adult season. The same actors are often contracted for school and adult shows. Lucille Wagner remembers the addition of an adult season as a desire to share the company's pride and satisfaction with the whole community. A family audience was invited to attend *The History Show II* in 1972 and the response was enthusiastic. It became obvious that adults would support this theatrical venture.

With greater financial support, the production schedule grew from two plays and 100 performances in 1972 to seven plays and 275 performances in 1976. Within four years of its existence, ATP had produced over thirty locally written plays. The school program which gave birth to the company remains its primary concern. Although school children form a captive audience, the school boards will only support quality programs. ATP has consistently proven itself in this area.

Quality in a company begins with the artistic director. Douglas Riske is constantly searching for good scripts which

141

Lucille Wagner, Administrative Director of Alberta Theatre Projects of Calgary

usually work for a variety of age groups. He believes that all theatre (no matter what age the audience) must provide art. Riske favoured expansion to include an adult subscription season because it offered a greater variety of styles and dramatic forms. The longer, adult productions made greater demands on the whole company.

Alberta Theatre Projects is in the business of producing historical drama both for young people and adults. The scripts are chosen as good drama, not for history lessons. The themes often deal with the struggles of anonymous individuals and historical figures who first inhabited or immigrated to Canada. One senses real people behind the characters. Bruno Bettleheim stated:

> Factual knowledge profits the total personality
> only when it is turned into "personal
> knowledge."[2]

Personal knowledge comes from being able to identify with and care about the characters and issues. Meaning comes through the audience sorting out the conflicts personally. If the play challenges the audience beyond its present intellectual, emotional and imaginative levels, then it has something of value to offer.

Examples of such historical plays produced by ATP include *Under the Arch, Boy Who Has a Horse, A Very Small Rebellion, The Judgement of Clifford Sifton, Cyclone Jack* and *The Day Jake Made Her Rain.* One of the most challenging plays for six to nine year olds is *Madwitch* by Paddy Campbell. It is a finely crafted drama about the effects of prejudice in a community on the prairies before World War II. An audience of children can easily identify with feelings about an old Indian woman whom children tease and taunt onstage. There are adults who represent the rational and irrational attitudes to "Madwitch" or Mary. There is the Nazi threat in Europe and possible prejudice against a German member of the community. *Madwitch* offers an enlightening view of human nature struggling against its own prejudices. If one is to criticize the script, it is on the basis of brevity. It could be expanded in dialogue, given the same characters and conflict. Campbell writes on the premise that a performance should

Under the Arch *by Paddy Campbell was adapted by the author for elementary schools*

leave a child with questions. If there are none, then the play has failed. *Madwitch* poses many social and personal queries. It is historical drama for the young at its best.

Under the Arch is a musical entertainment, played to audiences from ten year olds to adults, using two versions. This historical revue, with book and lyrics by Paddy Campbell and music by William Skolnik, began as *The History Show* in 1972 and ended as a polished musical. Campbell's gift for satire fits well into a Victorian music hall form, presenting the evolution of Western Canada both from the native people's and the white point of view. *Under the Arch* is good musical theatre coupled with some painful revelations about the settling of the Wild West.

Bonnie Le May's *Boy Who Has a Horse* portrays the social and historical struggle of the Sioux nation as experienced by a young boy. Finished as hunters, resisting a change of economic and cultural lifestyle, the Sioux are doomed to starve and die unless they yield to the white man. This play incorporates the best features of both history and drama: a recreation of the past, characters which involve the audience, issues with an emotional impact on several levels.

144

A Very Small Rebellion, a stage fantasy about Louis Riel by Jan Truss, combines the poetic setting of the prairies with the struggle of a people for self-determination. Taken from a children's book of the same name, the author wanted "to convey a feeling of a sad and heroic figure... rather than a lesson." Truss employs poetic sounds and visual fantasy as integral parts of the script. She brings a special quality to the stage:

RIEL: I have loved my people
     I have led my people
     No crime.

VOICE: *whispering* Scott. Remember the blood
     of Scott.

RIEL: My people suffered.

     *It is dark. The INDIAN is standing stage
     front and side. RIEL, PRIEST and
     HANGMAN are in silhouette; the cast in
     the shadows.*

     Silence.

     The INDIAN moans.

     *The hanging is done with slow dignity.
     RIEL disappears down, as the noose rope
     unwinds.*

     Thinly, a coyote howls.

     The watchers cross themselves.

INDIAN: *moaning, then crying out*
     Riel. Louis Riel
     Leader of your people
     Your name shall never die.

During the last speech, the sound of prairie
birds is heard. As his words die, the thunder
of the buffalo herd is heard, deafening
then dying. [3]

There is a unity of the aural, visual and spoken elements. As in other ATP scripts, one is left with a feeling of the eternal battle for independence and self-realization against all odds.

Jan Truss wrote another play of hardship on the Western Canadian prairies: *The Judgement of Clifford Sifton.* In it, pioneers settling the West fight their own disillusion with the vast, great, glorious "Last Best West," as well as the harshness of the environment. Sound is used as a counterpoint to the struggle. The musical number, "Oh Won't You Please Come to Canada," composed by Quenten Doolittle, provides a lively contrast to the scenes of hardship, loneliness and depression:

> Oh won't you please come to Canada
> The Last Best West needs you (and you and
> you)
> Oh the sun always shines in Canada
> The skies are always blue (yes blue, yes blue,
> yes blue)
> We've got lots of lovely land to give away in
> Canada.... [4]

Compare this with the agonizing speech of a very pregnant young woman:

> Oh help me. Somebody. No one — nowhere to
> help me. Oh. Oh I'm afraid. Nobody. Nobody.
> Nothing. Nobody. And no wood left for the
> fire.... Oh dear — nothing to burn. I
> remember the Indians kept their fires going
> with buffalo — Oh. The pain.... But the
> buffalo are gone. Gone. He had to go away to
> work in the mines — to make money — to buy
> another horse — in time for seeding. Dolly died.
> Poor Dolly. Died with the foal still in her.
> THE PAIN. [5]

As well as nurturing new works, Riske also chooses established Canadian authors and plays.

Cyclone Jack by Carol Bolt is a personal portrait of Tom Longboat, marathon runner in the early 1900's. It is a good drama about Longboat and about exploitation of Indians in the North American culture. Despite a weak ending, this play deserves the many productions it has received across Canada.

Historical drama is an inflated term for the charming stories spun by W.O. Mitchell about life on the prairies. Alberta Theatre Projects produced *The Day Jake Made Her Rain* for its 1975-76 season. It was a highly successful tale about man combating the elements by faith, with a genuine flavour of the drought-ridden Saskatchewan farms and the humour of farmhands. Young viewers can identify with the kid as well as all the other issues in this wonderful drama, which could not fail but touch anyone, especially as directed by Douglas Riske.

Another powerful production was of *1837: The Farmers' Revolt* by Rick Salutin and Theatre Passe Muraille. It was originally an adult play, edited for junior high school audiences. There is no reason to think that teenagers could not comprehend the theme of revolution. The pitfalls of the boring history lesson were avoided. The production engrossed students with its energy, wit and dramatic truth. Riske's direction made lively use of strong actors and a superb set design by George Dexter. This was theatre of high quality for an audience of any age.

A moderately successful script produced by ATP was *Pioneer* by Paddy Campbell. Despite the author's satirical humour, it has a difficult format. Approximately twenty scenes portray immigrants to Canada from various parts of the world. There is hardly time or detail in the short scenes to become intensely involved with any one thread in the story. It works as a series of documentary portraits, but is not the best historical drama Campbell could write.

Similarly, *Roads, Rails and Riders* by James Gibson is a plethora of facts, with static monologues and descriptive narrative which might be good history, but makes deadly drama. The facts of early pioneer life are given too prosaically. The dialogue lacks conciseness, surprises or dramatic metaphor. Historians and dramatists have very different goals and skills.

The criteria generally evident in ATP's choice of scripts

The Day Jake Made Her Rain by W.O. Mitchell; designed by Grant Guy. Attention to realistic, accurate and evocative design can often be expected from Alberta Theatre Projects.

appear to be: good writing, Canadian author and setting, depiction of the joys and sorrows in the historical evolution of the land. There has been particular emphasis on the Canadian prairie experience. One also finds a common thread of concern with social issues and injustices which caused human pain and suffering: farmers' revolt, prairie droughts or exploitation of the Indian.

A theatrical experience for adults stands on its own: there is no formal preparation or follow-up for members of the audience. Not so with productions for schools in Canada. Some educators see theatrical experiences as means to an end. The form must fit in with educational objectives and philosophy. They expect it to correlate with the child's growth, which is measurable or clearly evident. Many teachers want the children to externalize what they learned by going to the theatre. Depending on one's educational philosophy, this may have validity, but it assumes that young people need "assistance" assimilating art. A good artistic experience offers different insights to different audience members. If we "help" the child see the play from "our" point of view, does he have a chance to assimilate the play and make it his own? Bruno Bettleheim believes that we do a disservice if we ask for a conscious analysis or if we rush the child away from the story.

He is talking about fairy tales, but the same holds true for all good drama. A good historical play especially offers material to the young person which is both emotional and rational. Urging a child to express the meaning should allow for either or both of these areas. It would be a barren experience if a child only learned historical facts from theatre without the human complexities surrounding them.

How does a company bridge the dual goals of art and education? School boards who subsidize ATP see the "outing" to the Canmore Opera House as part of the school program. Some educators have the need to justify and rationalize attendance at plays. Others would consider it pointless or potentially destructive. Nevertheless, ATP responds to such expectations by providing preparation and follow-up as a responsibility to schools.

Alberta Theatre Projects has tried three ways of dealing with preparation or follow-up. First, a follow-up program was co-ordinated by a staff member; next, a "Theatre-in-Education" team carried out both preparations and follow-up; and the third approach has used video-cassettes. It should be remembered that an outing to the historic Canmore Opera House is in itself a "field trip."

In the first type of program, printed material from ATP states that the follow-up coordinator:

> Will expand upon the performance experience
> using creative drama, music, and art to
> reinforce the knowledge gained from the
> performance.[6]

For *Madwitch*, the written handout to teachers includes questions which are cognitive, ("What did Joanie tell her parents when she lost her pencil case? Did she tell the truth?"); others ask the child for emotional responses based on the story ("How do you feel when you move into a new neighbourhood?"). It is clear though, in keeping with the written objective of the follow-up, that the questions suggested to the teacher are more cognitive than effective — "to assist the teacher in attaining a total learning experience."[7]

In 1974, a significant change took place in the preparation. ATP hired a team of four who became the Theatre-in-

Education Division. This TIE team is *not* like its English relative with the same name. Difficulties arose with the concept at ATP and it may have been partly due to the confusion between the two. The English version employs actor-teachers who use theatre towards educational ends:

> It was conceived as an attempt to bring the
> techniques of theatre into the classroom, in the
> service of specific educational objectives.[8]

The ATP directors see as their primary goal providing good theatre, with the secondary aim of assisting teachers to make the artistic experience meaningful in educational terms. After all, the school boards substantially subsidize ATP's program for young audiences.

The TIE team, during its brief existence at ATP (1974/75), did design an extensive program of preparation and follow-up, providing notes, bibliographies and lesson plans for the teacher to use. The TIE team's preparation is described:

> AIM: As an "aware audience" the student's
> experiences at the theatre will be
> enriched as a result of our visit.

> OBJECTIVES: The students will understand
> the "job" of the audience in attendance
> at a live theatre performance.

> The students will understand theatre as
> a collaborative art form.

> The students will see the theatre from
> the point of view of various theatre
> artists. (Director, playwright, designer,
> *etc.*)

> PRESENTATION:

> 1. Introduction — The Theatre-In-Education team
>   member will introduce him/herself and
>   explain his/her function.

— Our presence in the schools
is to build a relationship for
an on-going process, *i.e.,* the
development of the indiv-
idual as an active participant
in live theatre.

2. Personal experiences with audience
   situations, *e.g.,* football game, TV
   — Analysis of experiences,
   expectations on the part of
   the audience and others
   involved in the event.
   — What does each bring to the
   experience?

3. Comparison of the theatre experience with
   those other audience events.
   — Contrast with other performances through other
   media.

4. What theatre artists bring to the event.
   — As time permits, a discussion
   of the "roles" of various
   artists.
   — The director.
   — The designer.
   — The actor.

5. What the playwright brings to the theatre.
   — Conflict.
   — Point of view.
   — When director meets
   playwright.

NOTES:

Throughout the discussion in the classroom, we
will be moving from the general situation to the

specific, *i.e.*, the focus will be on the students' attendance of a live performance of *Under the Arch* at the Canmore Opera House in Heritage Park.[9]

The packets circulated to teachers were voluminous with ideas and references, when compared with much shorter mimeographed materials accompanying the video-cassettes. The follow-up suggestions for *Under the Arch* included lesson outlines for five different units, which might be developed towards a documentary theatre experience. These included sequences in: Sound-Music, Movement, Puppets, Creative Writing and Improvisation. There were suggestions for working on different themes, and ways that other specialists (Music, Physical Education, Art and Language) could assist the drama teacher. The TIE team offered rich ideas for extending the script material. Presently, ATP lacks the financial or human resources to handle both the production of plays and leadership in creative drama. That is what brought ATP to using video-cassettes. Each play has a specially designed videotape which is made available to teachers for viewing in school. With this system there is no specialist in charge, or preparation or follow-up. There need only be a house manager for the performances.

By accepting video for its own strength, ATP does not try to duplicate with personal visits which used to accompany preparation. Rather, each tape provides self-contained information or experience. On the *Jake* tape, W.O. Mitchell informally chats about the process of creative writing, with the underlying message to students that they can do it too. Then the director, the designer and an actor comment on the process of play production. The ten-minute tape accompanying *The Judgement of Clifford Sifton* presents authentic period photographs with readings from the diary of an immigrant to Western Canada. It evokes the times and hardships of such transmigration. Another tape wholly consists of a National Film Board film about William Lyon Mackenzie, to introduce: *1837: The Farmers' Revolt*. ATP also provides mimeographed suggestions for follow-up. For *1837*, the ideas centre around Canadian forms of government. Preparation for *Clifford*

152

1837: The Farmers' Revolt *by Rick Salutin and Theatre Passe Muraille;* designed by George Dexter, *illustrates Alberta Theatre Projects frequent ingenious use of small and limited facilities*

Sifton suggests discussion and writing on the themes of emigration and immigration.

Within five years ATP grew so rapidly that it employed thirteen people in administrative roles, as well as twenty-four, plus cast, to work on productions. The large staff overtaxed the budget, particularly with inflationary costs. The company was forced to cut both administrative and production staff, as well as the whole TIE team. Other positions became part-time. This lightened the budget considerably. The fiscal price ATP had paid for its growth is instructive. It was founded in 1972 with $16,000.00 from the Local Initiatives Program. By 1973, the budget increased to $124,000.00 from LIP, the provincial Educational Opportunities Fund, corporate and private donors. In 1974 the LIP program was dropped and the two school boards helped to finance the company. By the 1976-77 season, the school program was around $110,000.00, not counting administrative costs. The budget for both young and adult seasons in 1977-78 was approximately $343,000.00.

Apart from the cutback in staff, renewed funding campaigns were necessary. The program for young audiences

153

does not seem to have suffered as a result. Lucille Wagner finds corporate fund-raising for children's programs relatively easier than for the adult season. Due to heightened efforts by ATP's board of directors the accumulated deficit has been receding from $122,053.00 in 1976 to $68,488.00 in 1977. The debt was retired by 1979: quite a feat in these days of economic crises.

The financial picture illustrates the fertile growth, the production list shows the exciting artistic achievements, and the company's reputation proves Alberta Theatre Projects' success by any standards. The future promises a continuing good record. There is no reason to suspect a change in the preference for material with a social conscience — giving a sympathetic view of early Canadians as "victims" (Margaret Atwood's image in *Survival*), of geography, seasonal hardships or political turmoil. This strong thread underlying ATP's work is not simply there for "educational" reasons, but because the directors are personally committed to the Western Canadian landscape. If scripts do not meet these criteria, ATP will certainly continue its policy of searching out and commissioning authors.

More ideal is Douglas Riske's desire for a resident playwright. Commissions rarely give enough advance time to develop the script. A writer-in-residence is paid a salary to work on location. A program functioned at ATP with John Murrell for one adult season and Sharon Pollock, writing scripts for young audiences, for two seasons.* But Riske claims it is difficult to find an experienced and dedicated playwright to work on scripts for the young.

Another question for the future is space. Charming and historically appropriate the Canmore Opera House may be, but its drawbacks are also obvious: 165 seats, distance from the city, small stage and limitations in other technical areas. Should the company look for another space? If offered a home in a projected Calgary performance centre, would this benefit ATP? What would be the implications of greater seating capacity in a different architectural environment? Douglas Riske says he would limit young audiences to 200, but not the

---

*The two plays written by Pollock for young audiences were *The Wreck of the National Line Car* and *Chautauqua Spelt E-N-E-R-G-Y*. (Z.B.)

adult audience. Are there alternative places in the city which may be better suited? In the future Alberta Theatre Projects must consider answers to these questions.

We will take you on a journey, a journey of
jeopardy and joys, with jesters and juggernauts
and even a few jobbermowls (look that one up).
We stand in the shadow of plough and pioneer,
of whiskey and wanderlust. The shadow grows
long over our polluted plains and soon will
disappear. Come back with me, if you dare, and
if you care, for what you are is what you were
and cannot be brushed off your Sunday coats
like so much dust. . . . [9]

Footnotes

1. Campbell, Paddy and William Skolnik. "Under the Arch," *Canadian Theatre Review (CTR 10)*, Spring, 1976, p. 52.
2. Bettleheim, Bruno, *op. cit.*, p. 54.
3. Truss, Jan. *A Very Small Rebellion.* An unpublished version of the script as produced by ATP, pp. 37D-38A. This script has been published by Playwrights' Co-op, Toronto, 1979.
4. Doolittle, Quenten, Composer for *The Judgement of Clifford Sifton*, Playwrights' Co-op, Toronto, 1979.
5. Truss, Jan. *op. cit.*, pp. 37D-38A.
6. Follow-up for *Madwitch*. Unpublished Circulated Mimeographed Sheets, Alberta Theatre Projects, 1973.
7. *Ibid.*
8. O'Toole, John, *op. cit.*, "Preface."
9. Classroom Preparation for Production of *Under the Arch*, Unpublished Mimeographed Notes, Alberta Theatre Projects TIF. Division, 1975.
10. Campbell, Paddy and William Skolnik, *op. cit.*, p. 53.

Part Three
Impressive Beginnings
Petite histoire des grands événements en théâtre pour les jeunes au Québec
by Hélène Beauchamp

Impressive Beginnings

Theatre for young audiences has developed rapidly in Québec in the past eight years, following the emergence of theatre collectives across the province, the construction of regional cultural centres and the boost of Expo '67. Some companies already engaged in the field prior to 1970 have maintained their initial thrust, others have gradually enlarged their ranks or been replaced by similar groups. Since 1970 quite a few companies and theatre collectives[1] have been formed whose work is totally or partially directed towards theatre for the young. This rapid growth inevitably brought about lively discussions on children and the theatre, and resulted in the emergence of different methods of work and theatrical ideologies. In writing about theatre for young audiences in Québec, one must take into account the many forms which it has taken. One must also make choices. I have chosen to discuss the work of those companies and collectives which are known inside as well as outside Québec, and whose research has spurred the development of theatre for youth. About each of these I will give an historical sketch, from inception to 1978, as well as an appraisal, inevitably personal and subjective, of their most significant productions and activities.

The most far-reaching commitment towards young audiences has been maintained by La Nouvelle Compagnie Théâtrale,[2] presently directed by Gilles Pelletier and Françoise Gratton. High school audiences come from as far as Québec City to their theatre in Montréal. Their productions since 1964 have been largely from the classical repertoire. This specialization does not preclude, as we shall see, considerable openness to other possibilities. The stability of the N.C.T. contrasts, however, with the ups and downs that other resident companies have weathered in Montréal and Québec City.

Other groups, performing to audiences scattered through the province in areas not fortunate enough to have resident companies, have suffered from the lack of efficient cultural policies. When touring outside the province, they have often been invested with the role of ambassadors. Bilingualism, the French language, a specific culture, an extensive folklore are values meant to be shared. It is from this point of view that the achievements of Les Jeunes Comédiens and of Le Théâtre des Pissenlits will be analyzed.

159

Most important to the development of theatre for young audiences, however, is the research done by artists who explore the realm of children and create plays that reflect their findings. If Micheline Pomrenski, director of Le Théâtre Soleil, derived her "théâtre d'expression" from the Brian Way method,[3] Monique Rioux and La Marmaille innovated in their approach to children and to children's theatre through workshops and plays. The technique has been labelled "jeux d'expression dramatique" and evolved through years of experimentation.

Québec is also benefiting from the work of many other theatre collectives actively involved in children's theatre, which have re-grouped as a working committee of L'Association Québécoise du Jeune Théâtre. They organize yearly festivals since 1974 and meet regularly to exchange research findings. These activities continue to give the necessary impetus and stimulation to the development of writing, acting and producing. The field of endeavour is vast and each production is rich in finding new definitions and appropriate forms of theatre for the young.

Theatre in Residence

Professional adult companies in Montréal indicated their readiness to perform for young audiences prior to 1967. Le Théâtre-Club, for instance, founded and directed by Monique Lepage and Jacques Létourneau, presented afternoon matinees of classical plays to high school students during their regular seasons from 1960 to 1963. In 1964, Le Théâtre-Club closed its doors, but at the same time La Nouvelle Compagnie Théâtrale was founded by Gilles Pelletier, Françoise Gratton and Georges Groulx. They chose specifically to cater to high school students. Their objective was twofold: bring students to the theatre and get them acquainted with classical plays. So from 1964 to 1968 Racine, Marivaux, Goldoni, Molière, Shakespeare, Musset, Chekhov and Sophocles were offered weekdays in Le Gesù, a hall with 860-seat capacity located in the heart of Montréal.

The 1968-69 season marked the opening of the N.C.T. to Québec authors. *Un Simple soldat*, the most "classical" of the plays written by Marcel Dubé, a well-known and prolific writer of the 1960's, was staged along with *Volpone* and *Le Jeu de l'amour et du hasard*. Moreover, *Salomon*, the work of two students, André Lamarre and Normand de Bellefeuille, chosen from the many

Un simple soldat by *Marcel Dubé, produced by La Nouvelle Compagnie Théâtrale of Montréal in 1968*

received for the first annual playwriting competition sponsored by the N.C.T., was given equal treatment. The contest was continued until 1972 as was the policy of producing established Québécois dramatists.

To be chosen for the regular season, a play by a Québec playwright has to be deemed "classical." The criteria for this are not that clear. *Le Cri de l'engoulevent* by Guy Dufresne (1959) will probably be forgotten as years pass, whereas *A toi, pour toujours, ta Marie-Lou,* by Michel Tremblay (1971) may well survive. *Ines Pérée et Inat Tendue* by Réjean Ducharme is a strange play by a talented novelist while *Bousille et les justes* by Gratien Gélinas is just short of melodrama. Nevertheless, the N.C.T. fulfills an important service to Québec drama by remounting plays five, ten or fifteen years after their creation and by giving students the opportunity to look into their own (if sometimes quite recent) cultural past. In programming its seasons to include two or three world classics and one Québécois play, the N.C.T. functions along the same lines as some Montréal adult companies and particularly Le Théâtre du Nouveau Monde.[4]

The N.C.T.'s style of production is quite coherent with its choice of repertoire. Professional actors are hired who are regularly cast in "adult" productions and who seem to appreciate the spontaneity of young audiences and their sometimes boisterous reactions. Directors and designers are selected from among the best in the profession. Usually[5], the plays are staged in their social, historical and political contexts, though not necessarily as they would have been originally presented. For *La Ménagerie de verre* in 1973, the walls of the theatre were covered with phrases and quotations so as to evoke the pre-war atmosphere in the southern United States; *En attendant Godot* in 1971 was performed on a revolving stage; *Mademoiselle Julie*, in 1976, translated into contemporary images and ideas the reality of 1888. Some short Chekhov plays in 1978 were introduced by Russian folksongs sung to the accompaniment of an accordion and also by an illustrated talk on Chekhov, Stanislavski and the Moscow Art Theatre.

Such classics, from Québec and elsewhere, are chosen mainly as examples of what dramatic writing is about, because they are significant signposts or constitute models of different styles. Direct correlation between the plays and current events are rare. When by chance it occurs, it is never underlined. The N.C.T.'s aim then is to give students a knowledge of theatre, of its history, its authors and its techniques.

To further enhance its selection the company inaugurated another kind of program in 1971: Opération-Théâtre. Specifically aimed at the twelve to fourteen age group, it was designed as an initiation to the theatre. Québec authors were commissioned to write plays about the theatre: Roland Laroche and Gilles Marsolais for *Opération-Théâtre* in 1971-72, Jean Barbeau for *Le Théâtre de la maintenance* in 1972-73, Renée and Robert Gurik for *Op-production* in 1973-74. Michel Garneau, Claude Roussin, Jacques Duchesne, authors who do not specialize in writing for young audiences, saw some of their works produced in this context. Others who regularly work with theatre collectives were also given this opportunity. *C'est tellement cute, des enfants*, by Marie-Francine Hébert, was presented by La Marmaille and *Impromptu chez Monsieur Pantalon*, by Louise Lahaye, was performed by La Rallonge.

This meant a new and vital opening of the N.C.T. to authors and theatre collectives, a practice which will no doubt be continued in the Fred Barry Hall.[6] In 1978, numerous events have

André Le Coz

Le Théâtre de la maintenance *by Jean Barbeau, produced by La Nouvelle Compagnie Théâtrale of Montréal in 1973*

163

already taken place in this experimental theatre (or "atelier N.C.T.") under the direction of Jean-Luc Bastien. Photos of groups and authors specializing in theatre for young audiences adorn the entrance, inviting young and less young alike to enter. To encourage theatre-going and to foster its well-established relationship with educators, the N.C.T. brings out for each production a teacher's guide: *les Cahiers de la Nouvelle Compagnie Théâtrale*. Each play is studied from historical, theatrical, sociological and literary points of view. At first, the booklets were distributed solely to teachers, but since 1970 this important documentation is available to anybody who wishes to acquire them.

Since its inception La Nouvelle Compagnie Théâtrale has been faithful to its goals and successful, in spite of financial and other difficulties, in maintaining its program for young audiences. The following data testify to this record: [7]

1965-1966:	53,500	spectators
1970-1971:	102,460	spectators
1976-1977:	31,000	subscriptions to the series of three plays;
	30,000	subscriptions to two - "Opération-Théâtre";
Total subsidy	:	$332,000.00
Subscriptions	:	$248,000.00
Sale of booklets	:	$ 11,000.00

Over the years, Gilles Pelletier and Françoise Gratton have consolidated their links with educators and young spectators. They understand not only that the classics are basic and should be performed in a highly professional manner, but also that contemporary creations, by individuals or collectives, are essential and should occupy a most important place in the planning of a season.

Le Théâtre du Rideau-Vert, founded in 1948, inaugurated its Théâtre-Jeunesse in 1967, when it opened the doors to its new theatre on Saint-Denis Street in Montréal. André Cailloux was then given the responsibility of developing this section and since then he has produced many of his own scripts[8], as well as some written by Patrick Mainville, Roland Lepage and Marcel Sabourin. Those works as well as the puppet shows prepared by

Il était une fois en Neuve-France by *Diane Bouchard, performed by Le Théâtre l'Avant-Pays of Montréal in 1978*

Pierre Régimbald and Nicole Lapointe were, until recently, presented on Sunday afternoons to audiences composed of children and adults.

One show with puppets and one with actors were thus produced each year. They were either based on legends or consisted of stories written according to the classical structure of the fairy tale. Invariably, the young spectators witnessed a hero going through a series of adventures and difficulties, being helped by a fairy or magician and surmounting his trials. In 1977-78, for example, *Pinocchio* was presented with imaginatively constructed puppets. But the moral code sustaining the story (one must tell the truth or one's nose will grow out of all proportions; one must go to school, otherwise one will be subjected to the humiliating experience of theatre) was kept unchanged and therefore unchallenged.

Fantasy, imagination and the marvellous, as well as myths and legends, do have a place in children's theatre. However, one does not create interesting children's theatre just because one uses the marvellous or writes according to traditional patterns. Needless

165

to say, "television children" do not have the same frame of reference as the Black Forest youth of the Middle Ages. They still feel joy, fear, sadness, compassion, jealousy and love, but their words, images and wave-lengths have changed. A recent witness to this is the very interesting play written by François Depatie and presented by Le Gyroscope in the Fred Barry Hall of the N.C.T. *En écoutant le coeur des pommes* seems to come from children's imagination, from inside their eyes and dreams, from the inner circle of their own games, and from our own epoch.[9]

Le Théâtre du Rideau-Vert, probably to avoid a certain sclerosis and also to make way for new trends, has wisely decided, for its 1978-79 season, to invite Le Théâtre de l'Avant-Pays with its production of *Il était une fois en Neuve-France*. The play, based on French-Canadian legends, is excellently done with puppets, manipulated "at sight" by actors actively involved in the plot and with the characters. Moreover, children in the Montréal region now have a choice of theatre activities during the weekends. Le Théâtre de Maisonneuve (Place des Arts), Le Conventum (Montréal) and Le Pont-Tournant (Beloeil) regularly produce quality professional productions for young spectators on Saturdays and Sundays.

In Québec City, Les Productions pour Enfants de Québec attracted 16,000 primary school children to L'Institut Canadien for its two productions of the 1977-78 season: *Histoire aux cheveux rouges* by the French author Maurice Yendt and *Qui est le roi?* by the Québécoise Nicole-Marie Rhéault. The theme was racism and both productions were highly professional in realization: lighting and sound were integrated, sets and costumes contributed to the creation of a specific atmosphere and the actors performed in a stylized fashion that further enhanced the meaning.

This newly formed group (September, 1976) was certainly welcome in Québec City where Le Trident, the resident company of Le Grand Théâtre de Québec, had discontinued its activities for young audiences. The tradition here in children's theatre is also quite strong, as it goes back to 1964 when Pauline Geoffrion founded Le Théâtre pour enfants de Québec (1964-69). This company produced plays written by Québec City authors (Pierre Morency[10], Jean Royer, Patrick Mainville and Monique Corriveau, a well-known writer of children's literature), directed, acted and designed by local artists (André Ricard, Marc Legault,

Marc Doré and others)[11]. They played in college and church halls, at Laval University, in L'Estoc, Québec City's experimental theatre, in L'Institut Canadien, and in about 1968 started touring schools in and around the city:

Le Théâtre pour enfants de Québec
1964-69

18 productions
329 performances
75,000 spectators

Total budget : $43,800
Of which $25,000
                      was paid to the artists

In 1970, however, with the building of Le Grand Théâtre de Québec, a new company was formed: Le Trident. It incorporated the three existing ones (L'Estoc, Le Théâtre pour enfants de Québec and Le Théâtre du Vieux Québec) and it was to serve repertory, experimental and children's theatre. It respected this mandate and presented a total of seven plays for youth. The early productions, *Faby en Afrique*, *Badaboum I* and *Badaboum II*, were performed on weekends only. They attracted an average of 7,000 spectators. In 1973, under the direction of Pauline Geoffrion, the plays were offered to the school boards and the attendance quadrupled.

In 1974 and 1975, François Depatie directed two of his own plays for Le Trident: *Le Cadran et le cerf-volant* and *Luclac dans l'Infini*. Poetic and lightly surrealistic, like dreams and fairy tales, the plays are nevertheless closely linked to the reality of today's children. As the following figures suggest, they were highly appreciated:

Le Trident - Fifth season - 1974-75
5 adult plays   2 children's plays
45,560 spectators   32,568 spectators

However, the lack of an artistic policy concerning the choice of texts and of styles quickly led to an impasse. In the spring of 1976, Le Trident abandoned its productions of plays for the young. It is

Le Fou de l'île by Félix Leclerc, adapted by Denis Chouinard, produced by Les Productions pour enfants de Québec of Québec in 1979

then that Louis-Marie Lavoie, Christian Martineau, Dominic LaVallée, Mathieu Gaumont, Nicole-Marie Rhéault and others who had been involved in Le Trident's productions, took it upon themselves to found Les Productions pour Enfants de Québec. Their plays are performed in a comfortable theatre so that—they argue—audiences can fully experience the special event of a production complete with sound, lights, sets and costumes. For them, children's theatre is a constant search for meaningful texts, effective techniques and stimulating workshops to take into the schools whose students have seen their plays. This gives them feedback and an essential dialogue is maintained. It is my opinion that permanent companies should take particular care not to become estranged from their audiences. The technical possibilities of the theatre building need not create a gap between actors and spectators.

Theatre on the Road

Touring has always been a necessity for companies playing to young audiences. To reach their specific public they go into schools with few props and costumes, knowing that they will

168

perform in a gymnasium with children sitting on the floor all around. But whenever "theatre" is brought *into* the schools an ambiguity arises as to its real purpose. Is it an artistic experience or an educational supplement? Even if the theatrical forms are undiluted, school acts in the role of the producer. Many discussions arose on this topic recently,[12] ranging from censorship in schools (of language and sometimes of ideas) to the challenge of out-of-school touring.[13]

It is my opinion, however, that such tours are profitable to collectives and companies which have a strong foothold in a region or a city, who can identify themselves with a "home-base" and who prepare their productions with a specific audience in mind. This immediate public, however small, constitutes a valuable sounding board and can influence both the style of performance and the choice of ideas to be conveyed. Many theatre collectives in Québec have chosen to identify themselves with such publics and their plays therefore reflect specific regional realities. Witness Lacannerie in Drummondville, Le Parminou in Victoriaville, La Bebelle in Sherbrooke, La Marmaille in Longueuil. They essentially define themselves as regional theatre collectives even though some tour very extensively.[14] This was not the case for Les Jeunes Comédiens nor is it so for Le Théâtre des Pissenlits.

Originally, Les Jeunes Comédiens was formed with students from the French section of the National Theatre School in Montréal who were invited by the Manitoba Theatre Centre to present a play by Molière: *Le Mariage forcé*. This was in 1963. The following year other graduating students under the same name toured the high schools of Ontario and Québec with two Molière plays: *L'Amour médecin* and *L'Impromptu de Versailles*.

From 1966 to 1972-73 the company greatly varied its repertoire, presented plays as well as improvised collective creations under the direction of Jean-Pierre Ronfard. Its tours were organized jointly by the National Arts Centre and Le Théâtre du Nouveau Monde. During its last season it toured for thirty-two weeks.

Productions by Les Jeunes Comédiens were highly praised, both the classics and their own creations. I personally recall the vivacity of their acting, the extraordinary involvement they displayed in their individual roles, the imaginative props, costumes and sets they used. They certainly left memorable souvenirs to quite a few spectators across the country.

This company of graduating students which was renewed each year gradually came to be composed of actors who decided to stay together, to form a stable group and to define its artistic policies. The work became more and more experimental with such classics as *Ubu Roi* and *Don Quichotte*, and even though they still performed in high schools, colleges and universities, their aim, as it developed, was more research-oriented than playing for young audiences. And when Les Jeunes Comédiens talked about settling down and playing in Montréal, their natural home-base, the purpose of their company was defeated. It had been designed primarily as a touring group.

Le Théâtre des Pissenlits, founded in 1968 by Jean-Yves Gaudreault in Jonquière (Lac St-Jean), has also done extensive touring, playing to spectators all across Canada, the north-eastern United States and in Louisiana. They also toured in Québec and, until last year, gave their productions in Montréal theatres during Christmas holidays.

Their declared aim is to present professional theatre to youngsters; their belief is in theatre as a magical happening ("le seul miracle, c'est le théâtre"); and their quite legitimate ambition is to deal with the real preoccupations of their young audiences. Somehow, though, it seems that "theatre" in all of its technical aspects (from the organization of a trans-Canada tour to the building of a giant puppet) has overshadowed their research into young people's theatre in particular. Is it because the company has not taken the time to define its specific public or because it has failed in meeting it? Is it because it has put too much emphasis on the professionalism of sets and costumes and not enough on the essential contact between actor and spectator?

Some of the practices of Le Théâtre des Pissenlits may leave an observer wondering. Why should a play be introduced by a technician delivering a speech in which children are told to respect their neighbours as well as the theatre and not to make any noise? Why should actors, while playing, tell children repeatedly to sit down, not to move, to stay in place and not to talk? This atmosphere of discipline is highly negative.

Le Théâtre des Pissenlits has treated, basically, five themes in eight plays, the most important of which are *Les Ballons enchantés* (1975) and *Gulliver* (1976). For the first, ideas and dialogue were taken from a previous play (*Tit-Jean, Margoton et le mauvais*

170

Gulliver, *adapted by Pierre Fortin for le Théâtre des Pissenlits of Montréal in*
1978

génie,) itself adapted from Québec legends and added to excerpts
of an Andersen tale. The story, set partly in Québec and partly in
China(!), is full of action and events but neglects necessary moments of thought and reflection. Something is always happening
and characters keep on travelling while children "participate" by
answering the eternal "where did he go?" question. Moreover,
children (the few chosen ones) are asked to come on stage and to
improvise some imitation of a trade or craft. Those are meant to
be the birthday gifts of ambassadors to the Emperor of China.
Such characteristics are common to most of the scripts of Le
Théâtre des Pissenlits.

Gulliver, an adaptation of Swift's text that left very much to be
desired, consisted mainly of stage effects. The inhabitants of
Lilliput were played by actors rolling around on little stools while
the giants of Brobdinggnag were played by huge puppets. As a
result, the satirical aspects of the original text were lost and ideas,
feelings and emotions unfortunately left out. The 1978 production of *L'Enfant-Robot* was awkwardly written and allusions to
modern educational methods were often questionable.

The considerable financial support which Le Théâtre des Pissenlits benefits from (grants totalling $120,000) should have

171

given its directors ample opportunity to experiment in children's theatre, to research and instigate innovative scripts, to bring authors, directors, actors, designers, and musicians to the field. Unfortunately, little was done. Touring remains extensive and expensive, but children and the theatre do not really benefit from it. As Maurice Yendt wrote:

Theatre for young audiences is without traditions or a repertoire: therefore, it should be experimental and involved in research. It is through research that it will transcend being a minor genre and come into its own as a new and original form of dramatic expression.[15]

It is therefore a little awkward for a company and for subsidizing bodies to intensify the "showcase" form of touring when the basic research in the field is just starting to bear the first results.

Practical Research

It is obvious to anyone who has worked with theatre groups that research done within a company or collective rarely comes out under any other form than that of the production itself. Reasons for that abound and they are mainly financial, since performances are subsidized while research activities, which should precede and follow the actual productions, are not. How then is the practice to evolve, if those who create theatre for children cannot take time to research it?

In Québec, the research has mainly centred on play content and workshop techniques. Very little as yet has been done concerning the actor's work or the design of sets and costumes. More basic still are questions about children. Who are they? What are they? Where are they? Are they really the exact equivalent to the child hidden deep in every adult? Superiors, inferiors or equals? What do they understand and want to understand of what adults do and say? What is their own mode of communication? What is theatre for them?[16] Two quite different answers to this last question are provided by Micheline Pomrenski and by Monique Rioux.

Micheline Pomrenski founded Le Théâtre Soleil in 1971 and since then she has presented two plays a year on tour in the schools of Montréal and its suburbs, within a radius of up to thirty miles. Her specific approach was probably inspired by the Brian Way method,[17] but has since evolved independently. The main characteristic of Le Théâtre Soleil is to involve completely the spectators as "actors" in the production itself, thereby proposing a "théâtre d'expression" as Mrs. Pomrenski defines it. One month prior to the date of performance, an "animateur" comes to the school, invites the children and their teachers to participate in workshops on the theme of the play and explains how they can contribute to the production. This involves the whole school in preparations: documentation on the subject, the learning of songs, dances and dialogue, the making of some costumes and props. When the company comes into the school the whole gymnasium is converted into a specific setting into which the children's work is integrated. The plays, most of which are written by Micheline Pomrenski, consist mainly of elaborate outlines: highlights of a given story, dialogue, songs and dances. Numerous opportunities are provided in that outline for the children to participate, either collectively or individually. For example, a whole class can be called upon to perform its song or dance, or a young student, having learned a few lines, may be invited to engage in a short dialogue with one of the characters. Very often teachers and even the principal of the school will have roles to play.

The production for kindergarten to third grade students in 1977-78 was set in a forest where bears are holding their annual conference. They come from different countries to the meeting which is disturbed by the arrival of a fox-film-producer. The children are identified and costumed as "oursons Malais," "oursons Baribal" and "oursons à lunettes" and two teachers play assistants to the fox, who succeeds by the end in making all the bears into future film stars.

The play intended for the fourth to sixth graders was set in a parish hall in Abitibi in 1920. Other subjects can be gleaned from the titles of the plays: *La Forêt merveilleuse* (1973), *L'Abeille entre la ruche et la fleur* and *Expédition J.O. (objectif Jupiter)* (1974-75), *Une journée au marché: le Moussem* (1975-76) and *A l'ombre du cactus* (1976-77). Le Théâtre Soleil gives an average of two hundred and fifty performances each year, a "performance" providing two hours (or more) of costuming and playing to approximately 225 students. But is the company paying enough attention to the real

173

implications of organized participation and to the far-reaching effects of its themes?[18]

It could be argued that this form of participation, which takes place in a highly disciplined frame, is quite frustrating in that it is at the same time permissive and restricted, imposed but apparently spontaneous. It could also be said that Le Théâtre Soleil provides an excellent frame in which to revive the good old end-of-the-year presentation when each class, well rehearsed by a devoted teacher, would perform a little something to the school inspector, the parish priest and the proud parents assembled for the occasion. And, within such a strict frame of participation, can children be really creative? Furthermore, can they be critical about a production in which they are directly involved? Monique Rioux and her group, La Marmaille, have chosen to research children's theatre in quite a different manner and to communicate their results through diverse channels. Their basic method is the workshop and the end result may take the form of written publications, of a series of public workshops or of a play. Their constant aim has always been to know children better, to acquire an insight into their language and creativity and to invent appropriate techniques of communication with them through theatre. Theatre, then, is an instrument, a technique with which to work. Paramount are the ideas conveyed and the children involved in the process as creators, spectators and critics.

In November, 1972, Monique Rioux proposed to Le Centre d'essai des auteurs dramatiques, the professional organization of Québec playwrights, the creation of workshops that would bring together authors, actors and children. She then demonstrated her method, which consists in having children invent themes, characters, situations, dialogue, feelings, space and objects, thereby exercising their imagination and creativity. Actors are present in equal number and the children direct them to act out what they imagine, to give voice and body to their creations. Each child has a theatrical double, a sort of understudy who translates into theatrical reality what he or she has created. The authors involved can then work with this material and put together a play which will have been created by children and which is closely related to them. Such workshops and subsequent ones did indeed lead to the writing of scripts by Marie-Francine Hébert which were produced by La Marmaille, founded in January, 1973: *Le Tour du chapeau* (1973), *Tu viendras pas patiner dans ma cour* (1974) and

174

Daniel Meilleur of La Marmaille in a writers' workshop with children and actors in Montréal in 1973

C't'assez plate (1974).

The participation of Jeanne Leroux, actress and sociologist, in La Marmaille's research activities, no doubt contributed to the development of workshops held with children of different social backgrounds. The plays from these workshops clearly indicated that the differences in social origin were manifest in the characters, situations and dialogue created. It became evident that children were aware of—and receptive to—their immediate surroundings, that adults (including authors and actors) were inclined to undue protectiveness towards them, and that plays were often written to envelop children in an atmosphere of artificiality. What La Marmaille was then and still is saying, is that children are to be talked to, played with, listened to, lived with and that they grow up in the same world as adults do.

C'est tellement cute, des enfants, by Marie-Francine Hébert (1975)[19] was widely shown by La Marmaille and provoked many reactions on the part of parents and educators. The language used by children in the play is quite harsh and realistic, and the situations are not at all complimentary to adults. While children in the audience were happy to recognize some of their own doings on stage, quite a few parents and educators were probably thus initiated to the games children play once they are out of school and in the street. This led to thinking that adults could benefit greatly from theatre initially meant for children only, and that mixed audiences should be encouraged.[20]

Pourquoi tu dis ça?, by Claire LeRoux, Claude Roussin, Marie-Francine Hébert and Michel Garneau (1976), was produced after workshops done with youths of twelve and thirteen years of age. The play summed up their outlook on four different themes: the past, the school, the future and the family. It did not consist merely of descriptions but worked towards a critical approach to those realities, an approach which constitutes a recently developed style in the workshops of La Marmaille. The themes which the group now works on, range from toy commercials on television to children-as-learners in schools and aim at the emancipation of children in a society governed by adults. In workshops, children are left quite free to imagine, feel, verbalize and play around with such subjects. The main preoccupation of La Marmaille presently is that they be given the opportunity to be critical in an autonomous fashion.[21]

This important research, done by La Marmaille since 1972, has

Pourquoi tu dis ça? by *Claire LeRoux, Claude Roussin, Marie-Francine Hébert and Michel Garneau, written for La Marmaille and produced by la Nouvelle Compagnie Théâtrale of Montréal in 1976*

found its natural links with the work done by other collectives and companies, assembled into a working committee in 1975 by L'Association Québécoise du Jeune Théâtre.[22] This committee on children's theatre, whose members are collectives, companies and involved individuals, meets regularly to compare concepts of children's theatre, to discuss the activities of participating groups, to share information and to organize events of a provincial nature. The annual Festival du théâtre pour enfants du Québec, held every August, is under their jurisdiction and it remains the unique occasion for theatre groups to meet, present their own productions (to their peers as well as to children) and continue essential discussions on play content, writing and producing. Workshops held during the festivals prove to be fertile and influential. Groups regularly present for this annual meeting include: Lacannerie, from Drummondville, founded in 1973 by author Denis Lagueux; Le Théâtre du Cent-Neuf (1972) and La Bebelle (1974) from Sherbrooke; Le Théâtre de Carton, founded in 1972 in Longueuil; Le Théâtre de l'Oeil, founded in 1973, in Montréal; as well as La Grosse Valise (Montréal), Le Théâtre des Confettis (Québec), and Les Amis de Chiffon (Alma).

La Bicyclette, *a collective creation performed by Les Confettis in a Québec City school in 1978*

The close relationship established between groups working in the same field and united by a common purpose has grown to be very productive. Although they all agree that children are to be respected and treated as equals, they pursue research in different forms of theatre. Le Théâtre de l'Oeil, whose three members have just returned from a tour in Belgium, is experimenting in the symbolism and significance of puppets in theatre for children. La Bebelle has chosen the clown as a central medium of expression and tries to find ways to improve its performances. For these companies content is most important and their collective creations of the past two years have touched subjects like pollution, the segregation of the sexes brought about by family and school education and the importance of sharing. Le Théâtre de Carton creates plays which are highly critical of the emotional oppressions we are subjected to. Together these groups[23] have created a place where it is possible to meet, discuss, criticize one's work and learn. The following figures for the 1976-77 season provide an insight into their work:

	Performances	Spectators	Sales	Grants
Théâtre de l'Oeil	178	53,400	$25,000	$8,500
La Bebelle	60	24,000	9,600	2,700
Théâtre de Carton	160	46,384	30,800	5,000
La Marmaille	169	36,544	33,413	17,500

All, of course, has not been done. All, as a matter of fact, is just beginning. And there is vast potential to be tapped. If the governing and the subsidizing bodies realize that:

> Research is an essential part of production in theatre for young audiences (in signs, in languages, in ideas) and that research and production must be subsidized.
> Diversity in research, in writing and in production styles is to be encouraged.
> Policies of regional development are essential.
> A cultural centre for children, if ever constructed and financed, should be available to all groups and not placed under the jurisdiction of only one.

The writing of scripts must be encouraged through publication commissions and grants. Le Centre d'essai des auteurs dramatiques has published the summaries of approximately thirty scripts which it keeps at the disposal of theatre groups, educators and the general public. They have been written by individuals or created by collectives. Denis Lagueux, Marie-Francine Hébert, Michel Garneau, François Depatie stand out as the most promising authors.

Since 1972, the main stream of questioning has been related to the definition of "young audiences" and to the knowledge of children. It is now time to enquire into production techniques, into the theatrical translation of play contents as well as the use of specific styles.

If it all comes to pass, theatre for the young just might be the one form to incite the rest to action, fantasy, colour, imaginative forms and textures, songs and dances, puppets and clowns, trumpets and parades, reflection and content analysis, dreams and true reality, space, timing, rhythm—in short, to everything that might keep all theatre young and exciting.

Footnotes

1. "Theatre collective" in this text refers to a troupe of theatre artists/workers which produces plays collectively (text, administration, touring, acting, etc.); "company" refers to the theatrical organization in which an artistic director, seconded by a board of directors, chooses a play and hires actors, set and costume designers, technicians, etc. for a limited time and responsibility. It is important to note that two conservatories (one in Québec City, the other in Montréal), the National Theatre School (French section), two CEGEPs (in Ste-Thérèse and in St-Hyacinthe) as well as the theatre section of l'UQAM, train actors, theatre artists and technicians in the province of Québec.
2. I consider the article (le, la, l', les) to be part of the name of the company or collective and I therefore prefer not to translate it.
3. Brian Way is not as well known in Québec as he is in English-speaking Canada. Catherine Dasté is a more frequent reference.
4. Le Théâtre du Nouveau Monde gives a 50% reduction on regular tickets to high school students upon presentation of their identity card. The Centaur Company (English professional company) gives student matinees of those of its regular season plays which are considered to be of interest to that public.
5. Upon reflection on the plays that I have seen.

6. The Fred Barry Hall, located in the same building as the Denise Pelletier Theatre (875 seats) hold approximately 150 spectators. Both are located in the east of Montréal so as to boost cultural activities in that area.

7. I have selected, among available data, figures which attest to the importance of theatre for young audiences and its rapid growth, as well as to the evident discrepancy between budgets allotted to this activity and the number of spectators it attracts.

8. Les Editions Leméac in Montréal have published the following plays by André Cailloux: *Frizelis et Gros Guillaume* (1973), *Frizelis et la Fée Doduche* (1973), *l'Ile-au-Sorcier* (1974), *François et l'oiseau du Brésil with Tombé des étoiles* (1977).

9. This appreciation, of course, is mine, as this is how I experienced the play. *The Uses of Enchantment* by Bruno Bettleheim, analyzes the importance of the fairy tale for children, and the uses of the imagination and the marvellous as necessary sources of information. (Alfred A. Knopf, New York).

10. Two of his plays were published by Les Editions Leméac in Montréal: *Marlot dans les merveilles* (1975) and *Tournebire et le Malin Frigo with Les Ecoles de Bon Bazou* (1978).

11. The Conservatoire d'art dramatique de Québec was founded in 1958 but the actors and technicians trained there often had to come to Montréal to find work. In this respect companies based in Québec City were essential to the development of theatre in that city.

12. One discussion on the subject was formally organized by Le Centre d'essai des auteurs dramatiques where theatre artists met with educators. Le Centre d'essai des auteurs dramatiques is somewhat similar to the Playwright's Co-op in Toronto and is presently located at 211, rue St-Sacrement, Montréal.

13. Two theatre collectives in Sherbrooke are touring the parish halls this year, and Lacannerie in Drummondville decided to tour schools and community centres with the same productions, to compare results by the end of the season.

14. The Gaspé Peninsula, the north and south coasts of the St-Lawrence, Abitibi and the Saguenay regions are still quite difficult to reach and policies of decentralization have not been developed yet which would favour the founding of theatre groups in those regions.

15. As quoted in "Programme d'action artistique et politiques de fonctionnement, dit Manifeste" written by les Production pour Enfants de Québec, s.d. Translated by the editor.

16. Extensive summaries of discussions on those topics have been published by Le Centre d'essai des auteurs dramatiques in available booklets. Many chronicles, published in *Jeu, cahiers de théâtre*, Editions Quinze, Montréal, also contributed items for thought on these subjects.

17. Micheline Pomrenski's first experience in children's theatre was with the Youtheatre of Montréal, in a production of a Brian Way script. Youtheatre was founded in 1968 and celebrated its tenth anniversary season with *The Mirrorman* and *The Decision*, both written and directed by Brian Way; *Circus Kazoo*, a bilingual production written and directed by Wayne Fines, founder and artistic director of Youtheatre, and a

181

presentation of the Paul Gauguin Mime Company from Toronto. Youtheatre has produced quite a few plays, including most of the Brian Way scripts and others such as *Aladdin, Aesop's Fables* and *Historyherstory.* This professional company tours English schools in Montréal and up to 1977 also presented its productions in the Main Theatre on St-Laurent Boulevard.

18. Le Théâtre du Carrousel has chosen a similar pedagogical approach, but their themes are taken directly from the school curriculum and treated in quite a didactic fashion.

19. The play was published by Editions Quinze, Montréal, 1975. Les Editions Leméac in Montréal published *Une Ligne blanche au jambon* in 1974.

20. La Grosse Valise is actually doing *Faut pas s'laisser faire* to mixed audiences. This play, by Reiner Lücker and Volker Ludwig of the Grips Theatre for Children of Berlin, was adapted into Québécois by Odette Gagnon. It deals with single-parent families, of relationships between parents and children, and invites discussion on the role of children in the changing of social patterns. This play has been published in American, under the title, *Man oh Man*, by Jack Zipes, in *Political Plays for Children*, Telos Press, Saint Louis, 1976.

21. Monique Rioux, *L'Enfant et l'expression dramatique*, L'Aurore, Montréal, 1976; "La Marmaille, groupe de recherche" in *Jeu*, cahiers de théâtre, no. 4, hiver, 1977, Editions Quinze, Montréal, 1977, pp. 23-56.

22. On the development of this committee on children's theatre and of the annual festival, see my article, "Conditions du théâtre pour enfants", in *Jeu*, cahiers de théâtre, no. 2, printemps, 1976, Editions Quinze, Montréal, 1976, pp. 45-54.

23. Members of those collectives, as well as of La Marmaille and Le Théâtre Soleil, do not belong to L'Union des Artistes, the equivalent of Actors Equity. They do not, therefore, abide by its regulations. Instead, they have formed themselves into non-profit organizations. To define themselves and their work, member groups of L'Association québécoise du jeune théâtre have coined the expressions "troupe de métier" and "acteur de métier." For an analysis of the recent work of these collectives and companies, see my book: *Le Théâtre à la p'tite école*, published by le Service du théâtre du ministère des Affaires culturelles du Québec, 1978.

Afterword[1]

In retrospect, the summer of 1978 seems a fortuitous time to have completed the major part of this book. A number of significant events occurred during the year which affected its content and the future direction of theatre for young audiences in Canada.

Linda Gaboriau, a theatre officer of the Canada Council, finished her research and drafted the *Re-evaluation Report on Council's Assistance to Theatre for Young Audiences*. The Canada Council approved the report at its June, 1978 meeting, subject to funds becoming available, perhaps from the Secretary of State. Specific recommendations included: grant increases to established companies to compensate for expensive touring and to improve production quality; first-time grants to new eligible companies; a development program for Theatre for Young Audiences; a special touring program; a communications fund; a program for research projects and an increase in the budget of ASSITEJ Canada. The conclusion of this important document declared:

> The professional artists involved in Theatre for Young Audiences in Canada feel that TYA is at a turning point in its development. They believe TYA has more than proven its "potential" and has become a dynamic reality, producing exciting and innovative work that is a credit to Canadian Theatre at large.

> People in TYA say that this is a critical time for the Canada Council to grant coherent and significant support to an activity that is offering meaningful exposure to the professional, performing arts to hundreds of thousands of young Canadians every year.

> Those consulted believe that the additional funds requested to create a meaningful program of assistance to Theatre for Young Audiences is the minimum required to free TYA from the "poverty mentality" that has too long

dictated the salaries it can offer, the designs it can choose and the plays it can commission.

The price tag was over half a million dollars. It was hoped that the federal government would view the proposal as an appropriate way to acknowledge the UNESCO sponsored International Year of The Child, by endorsing the report in 1978 and implementing it in 1979.

Also in June, an event of unprecedented excitement and success occurred in Vancouver: the International Theatre Festival for Young People.* Eighteen companies from England, Australia, Japan and the Soviet Union, as well as from five Canadian provinces, performed in three gaily-striped tents on the grounds of Vanier Park. The sun shone and busloads of school children emptied in from the planetarium to fill the tents on weekdays. After school and on weekends, entire families arrived to enjoy the sun, the water and the ambiance, not to mention some excellent performances. One popular success was the Kaze No Ko company from Japan, returning for a second visit to Canada and charming all who saw them. Other highlights included flying a gigantic kite with the Davey family of Australia (The Round Earth Company,) Québécois artists applauding the English-speaking Kaleidoscope production of *Mon Pays*, a short history of "La Belle Province" created by director Elizabeth Gorrie, with Marie-Francine Hébert, and a standing ovation for the Green Thumb production of *Shadowdance*, directed by Yurek Bogajewicz. Hurrahs were in order for the organizers — Colin Gorrie as overall chief and Irene N. Watts as his assistant, and to Heritage Festival's Ernie Fladell for his vision and tenacity. The Green Room for players, the boat ride and final dinner, the thoughtfulness and attention to detail lavished on this event, all will make it a golden week in many memories for years to come. Even more exciting was the fact that three other Canadian cities had a chance to share in this celebration. As a preview to Vancouver,

*As this book goes to press, an equally ambitious event is planned for May 7-13, 1979. The Vancouver International Festival for Young People has expanded to include music and dance events, in addition to about two dozen theatre productions from Canada, the U.S.A. and Japan. As "The Greatest Little Traveling Supershow for Children" many of these productions visited other Canadian cities, large and small, under the auspices of the Canada Council's Touring Office and various local sponsors.

184

Calgary had hosted one foreign and three Canadian companies on tour. After Vancouver, selected troupes visited Montréal and Toronto. In every city, local companies were seen along with the visiting troupes to make up a week-long festival in each place. Press coverage was excellent and morale soared. When the delegation of ASSITEJ Canada attended the Sixth General Assembly in Madrid, it was evident how superior the performances in Canada had been.*

The new confidence was reflected in the elections of ASSITEJ Canada in Vancouver, as the companies themselves took over the National Centre, moving it from the University of Calgary to the National Arts Centre, under its newly-elected secretary, Magda Rundle. Joyce Doolittle was named honorary president and invited to continue her representation of Canada at international meetings. In Madrid, Canada retained its place on the International Executive Committee and Joyce Doolittle was elected to her third term as vice-president.

By the autumn, prospects looked less rosy. No action was taken on the Gaboriau brief in the office of the Secretary of State. The Touring Office of the Canada Council, instrumental in planning the Vancouver Heritage Festival for young people and hoping to make the tour for the International Year of the Child even more ambitious, was fighting off budget cuts. Linda Gaboriau's job as Theatre Officer in charge of Theatre for Young Audiences, vacant since spring, was filled by Magda Rundle. This meant moving the Canadian Centre for ASSITEJ for the second time in one year, this time to Victoria, B.C., to the care of the English co-president, Barbara McLauchlin. International representation was assumed by Ms. McLauchlin and Jean-Yves Gaudrealt, Francophone co-president, in November, 1978. As the *Canadian Theatre Review* has often noted, the closing of Canada's ITI Centre has meant losing regular information from abroad, including opportunities to perform as official Canadian entries in European festivals. Theatre for the young, on the other hand, has enjoyed a decade of regular ASSITEJ representation, annual publications and prompt announcements of invitations for companies or individuals to appear in other countries. One hopes that the current difficulties of ASSITEJ Canada will be overcome soon, so that future opportunities abroad may be promptly advertised, fairly allotted and well performed.

On Thursday, November 16, 1978, Sue Kramer, co-founder and co-artistic director of the Globe Theatre, died after a short illness of cancer, in Regina. At thirty-nine, Sue had already made a unique contribution to Canadian theatre, and especially to theatre for the young. The Globe had begun as a touring company for young people and had never looked back or down upon that first obligation. At meetings to give advice and to set priorities for Linda Gaboriau's report, Sue Kramer had been an eloquent advocate for artists performing for the young. Those of us who had known her since she first arrived in Canada, join her friends, her husband, Ken, small son and daughter, in mourning the loss of a remarkable human being.

It will be ironic if 1979, the Year of the Child, finds our professional theatre for children slipping back into the oblivion and apathy which has characterized the attitude of its adult public for so many years. The talent and dedication are undisputed. Now is the moment for a more enlightened funding policy to be implemented. The air of optimism generated last year could evaporate — as could the companies themselves — if general restraints on spending continue or worsen. Schools are important supporters of theatre for the young. School budgets are currently being curtailed and it is hard to imagine that the arts, particularly visiting artists, will not be affected by budget cuts. The Canada Council is under increasing attack and its overall budget has not been appreciably raised. With inflation, this amounts to a budget cut. Provincial support of young companies varies wildly from province to province and civic subsidy is seldom lavish. So funding remains a concern for the companies.

Quality continues to be — as it should be — a prime concern of each company. As we have tried to indicate in this book, the style of theatre for the young in Canada has moved from colonial borrowings of fairy tale plays from the U.S.A. and participation plays from England, to a more varied and indigenous Canadian style — or styles, we should say. For it is, in our opinion, one of the glories of the field that our style is so varied. It points to a career commitment by talented, dedicated and imaginative artists. The general rigidity and predictability of the seasons found in most regional theatres in the past eight to ten years, seems to have been avoided by the best of our young companies. Through research, the commissioning of scripts by established writers, and the creation of their own material, they have managed by and large to find their individual voices for the young of our nation. All this has happened under stringent financial conditions, mainly through very hard work and sacrifices by young artists. As these artists mature and the gap between them and the adult theatre widens, it is no longer acceptable to offer them low wages and lower esteem.

We have come to a crossroads in Canada for young people's theatre. Whether the road ahead will lead to higher quality and relevance and genuine artistic experiences for our young people, or to the discouragement of the best artists who cannot be expected to struggle against such odds, is up to all of us who care.

Joyce Doolittle
Zina Barnieh
Calgary, Alberta
April, 1979

Footnotes

1. Part of this afterword was adapted from an essay by Joyce Doolittle for the 1978 Theatre Yearbook, published by the *Canadian Theatre Review*.

Selected Bibliography

Books

Ariès, Philippe. *Centuries of Childhood,* Translated from the French by Robert Baldick, Random House, New York, 1962.

Atwood, Margaret. *Survival, A Thematic Guide to Canadian Literature,* Anansi, Toronto, 1972.

Bettleheim, Bruno. *The Uses of Enchantment,* Vintage Books, New York, 1977.

Bond, Edward. *Lear,* Methuen, London, 1972.

Brockett, Oscar. *The Theatre,* Holt, Rinehart and Winston, New York, 1964.

Bronfenbrenner, Urie. *Two Worlds of Childhood, U.S. and U.S.S.R.,* Simon and Schuster, New York, 1972.

Courtney, Richard. *Play, Drama and Thought,* Cassell, London, 1968.

Dewey, John. *Art as Experience,* Minton, Balch & Co., New York, 1934.

Donahue, John Clark and Linda Walsh Jenkins. *Five Plays from the Children's Theatre of Minneapolis,* University of Minnesota Press, Minneapolis, 1975.

Egoff, Sheila. *The Republic of Childhood, A Critical Guide to Canadian Children's Literature in English,* Oxford University Press, Toronto, 1975. (Second edition).

Farson, Richard. *Birthrites, A Bill of Rights for Children,* Macmillan, New York, 1974.

Ginott, Haim G., *Between Parent and Child,* Avon Books, New York, 1975.

Goldberg, Moses. *Children's Theatre: A Philosophy and a Method,* Prentice-Hall, Englewood Cliffs, 1974.

Holt, John. *Escape from Childhood,* Ballantine Books, New York, 1974.

Lesser, Gerald S. *Children and Television,* Vintage Books, New York, 1975

Lessing, Doris. *The Golden Notebook,* Panther Books, Frogmore, St. Alban's, Herts., 1973.

Maynard, Fredelle Bruser. *Raisins and Almonds,* Paperjacks, Don Mills, 1975.

New, William H., ed. Reaney, James, "Ten Years at Play,"
   Dramatists in Canada, U.B.C. Press, Vancouver,
   1972.
Opie, Iona and Peter Opie. *The Oxford Book of Children's
   Verse*, Oxford University Press, London, 1973.
O'Toole, John. *Theatre in Education: New Objectives for
   Theatre—New Objectives in Education*, Hodder and
   Stoughton, London, 1976.
Phillips, Robert S., ed. *Aspects of Alice: Lewis Carroll's
   Dream-child as Seen through the Critics' Looking
   Glasses*, Vanguard Press, New York, 1971.
Reaney, James. *Apple Butter and Other Plays for Children*,
   Talonbooks, Vancouver, 1973.
Rockefeller, David, Jr. *Chairman of the Panel Report: Coming
   to our Senses*, McGraw-Hill, New York, 1977.
Schwartz, Eugene. "The Most Demanding Audience," *Theatre
   for Children, Adolescents and Youth*, Translated by
   Miriam Morton, Iskvsstro Press, 1972.
Siks, G.B. and Hazel Dunnington. *Children's Theatre and
   Creative Dramatics*, University of Washington Press,
   Seattle, 1968.
Smith, Janet Adam, compiler. *The Faber Book of Children's
   Verse*, Faber and Faber, London, 1972.
Woodman, Ross. *James Reaney*, Canadian Writers #12, New
   Canadian Library, McClelland and Stewart,
   Toronto/Montreal, 1971.

Periodicals

Adilman, Sid. "Eye on Entertainment," *The Toronto Star*,
   November 10, 1975.
Anderson, John. "Psychological Aspects of Child Audiences,"
   Educational Theatre Journal II, December, 1950
Deverell, Rex. "Towards a Significant Children's Theatre,"
   Canadian Children's Literature, Number 8/9, 1977.
Devine, George. "Theatre for Children: Art That is Different,"
   World Theatre II, 1952.
Durbach, Errol. "Herod in the Welfare State: Kindermord in
   the Plays of Edward Bond," *Educational Theatre
   Journal*, December, 1975.

Frost, Ruth, "Notes on the Young Traveller," *Canadian Theatre Review (CTR 10)*, Spring, 1976.

Hanlon, Michael. "Henry Green and the Mighty Machine," *The Canadian*, Vol. I, No. 7, December 25, 1965.

Johnstone, Keith. "Acting," *Discussions in Developmental Drama*, No. 4. University of Calgary, February, 1973.

Kareda, Urjo. "Susan Rubes Fighting for Space to Live," *The Toronto Star*, February 6, 1975.

Kennedy, John. "Kid's TV: Who Does it Best?" *Chatelaine*, May, 1976.

Kupper, Herbert. "Fantasy and the Theatre Arts," *Educational Theatre Journal*, March, 1952.

Lambert, Betty. "On Writing Plays for Children; or, You Can't See The Audience from the Trapeze," *Canadian Children's Literature*, Number 8/9, 1977.

Lee, Dennis. "Roots and Play: Writing as a 35 Year Old Children," *Canadian Children's Literature*, Number 4, 1976.

Levy, Jonathan. "A Theatre of the Imagination," *Children's Theatre Review*, Vol. XXVII, Number 1, 1978.

Maddou, Ellen. "The Otrabanda Company," *The Drama Review*, American Theatre Issue, June, 1972.

McNamara, Brooks. "Stuart Sherman's Third Spectacle," *The Drama Review*. American Theatre Issue, June, 1972.

Mayer, Martin. "It Isn't Easy Being Educational — The Sesame Street Process," *Audience*, Volume 2, Number 2, March-April, 1972.

Rubes, Susan. "One Decade at a Time," *ASSITEJ Canada Newsletter*, Spring, 1976.

Shamberg, Michael. "Video — Literacy: Learning the Language of Television," *Horizon*, January, 1978.

Shapiro-Latham, Gloria. "Planit (A Community Action Game)," ASSITEJ *Canada Newsletter*, Spring, 1976.

Unpublished Materials

Eek, Nat. Closing Speech at the 5th International Congress of ASSITEJ. East Berlin, April 24, 1975.

Garbary, Evelyn. "An Innocent in the Theatre," Speech Delivered at the Acadia University Humanities Association, February, 1976.

Levy, Johathan. "Modern Plays in Period Styles — The Uses of Tradition in Children's Theatre," Address Given at the University of Calgary, February, 1972.

Lussier, Charles. "The Canada Council: The Principle of Excellence and Its Implications in a Democratic Society," Notes for an Address at Harvard University, 1977.

Plays for Young Audiences in English Canada

The following list includes scripts mentioned in this book:

Beissel, Henry. *Inook and the Sun*, Playwright's Co-op, Toronto, 1974.

Bolt, Carol. *Cyclone Jack*, Playwright's Co-op, Toronto, 1972.

Bolt, Carol. *Maurice*, Playwright's Co-op, Toronto, 1974.

Bolt, Carol. *My Best Friend Is Twelve Feet High*, Playwright's Co-op, Toronto, 1972.

Bolt, Carol. *Tangleflags*, Playwright's Co-op, Toronto, 1974.

Campbell, Ken. *Old King Cole*, Menthuen, London, 1975.

Campbell, Paddy. *Buckskin and Chaperos*, Unpublished, Produced by Alberta Theatre Projects, 1972.

Campbell, Paddy. *Chinook*, Playwright's Co-op, Toronto, 1973.

Campbell, Paddy. *The History Show*, Unpublished, Produced by Alberta Theatre Projects, 1973.

Campbell, Paddy. *In the Enchanted Box*, Unpublished, Produced by Allied Arts Centre, 1968.

Campbell, Paddy. *Madwitch*, Unpublished, Produced by Alberta Theatre Projects, 1974.

Campbell, Paddy. *Pioneer*, Unpublished, Produced by Alberta Theatre Projects, 1974.

Campbell, Paddy and William Skolnik. *Under the Arch, Canadian Theatre Review (CTR 10)*, Downsview, Spring, 1976.

Chorpenning, Charlotte, E. *Cinderella*, Anchorage Press, New Orleans, 1940.

Chorpenning, Charlotte, E. *The Emperor's New Clothes*, Samuel French, New York, 1959.

Chorpenning, Charlotte, E. *The Emperor's New Clothes*,

Chorpenning, Charlotte, E. *Hans Brinker and the Silver Skates*, Children's Theatre Press, Anchorage, Kentucky, 1938.

Chorpenning, Charlotte, E. *The Indian Captive*, Children's Theatre Press, Anchorage, Kentucky, 1937.

Deverell, Rex. *The Copetown City Kite Crisis*, Playwright's Co-op, Toronto, 1974.

Deverell, Rex. *Sarah's Play*, Playwright's Co-op, Toronto, 1975.

Deverell, Rex. *The Shinbone General Store Caper*, Playwright's Co-op, Toronto, 1977.

Deverell, Rex. *Shortshrift*, Playwright's Co-op, Toronto, 1974.

Deverell, Rex. *The Uphill Revival*, Playwright's Co-op, Toronto, 1977.

Fineberg, Larry and William Skolnik. *Waterfall*, Playwright's Co-op, Toronto, 1974.

Foon, Dennis. *Heracles*, Talonbooks, Vancouver, 1978.

Foon, Dennis. *Raft Baby*, Talonbooks, Vancouver, 1978.

Foon, Dennis. *The Windigo*, Talonbooks, Vancouver, 1978.

Garbary, Evelyn. *Glooscap and the Mighty Bullfrog*, Unpublished, Produced by Mermaid Theatre, 1974.

Garbary, Evelyn. *The Invisible Hunter*, Unpublished, Produced by Mermaid Theatre, 1974.

Garbary, Evelyn. *The Journey*, Unpublished, Produced by Mermaid Theatre, 1974.

Gibson, James. *Roads, Rails and Riders*, Unpublished, Produced by Alberta Theatre Projects, 1973.

Harris, Aurand. *Androcles and The Lion*, Anchorage Press, Anchorage, Kentucky, 1964.

Hébert, Marie-Francine and Liz Gorrie. *Mon Pays*, Unpublished, Produced by Kaleidoscope Theatre, 1978.

Hirsch, John. *Box of Smiles*, Unpublished, Produced by Manitoba Theatre Centre, 1963.

Jones, Elizabeth. *Glooscap's People. (Le Monde de Glooscap)*, Unpublished, Produced by Mermaid Theatre, 1974.

Kramer, Ken. *Shakespeare's Women*, Unpublished, Produced by Globe Theatre, 1971.

Lambert Betty. *The Riddle Machine, Contemporary Children's Theatre*, Edited by Betty Jean Lipton, Avon Books, New York, 1974.

LeMay, Bonnie. *Boy Who Has a Horse*, Playwright's Co-op, Toronto, 1974.

Mason, Timothy. *Robin Hood: A Story of the Forest, Five Plays from the Children's Theatre Company of Minneapolis*, Edited by John Clark Donahue and Linda Walsh Jenkins, University of Minnesota Press, Minneapolis, 1975.

McNair, Rick. *Beowulf*, Unpublished, Produced by Stage-Coach, Theatre Calgary, 1977.

Mitchell, W.O. *The Day Jake Made Her Rain*, Unpublished, Produced by Alberta Theatre Projects, 1976.

Mitchell, W.O. *The Devil's Instrument*, Simon and Pierre, Toronto, 1974.

Nicol, Eric. *Beware the Quickly Who*, Playwright's Co-op, Toronto, 1973.

Nicol, Eric. *The Clam Made a Face*, new press, Toronto, 1972.

Peterson, Len. *Almighty Voice*, The Book Society of Canada Ltd., Agincourt, 1974.

Pollock, Sharon. *Chautauqua Spelt E-N-E-R-G-Y*, Unpublished, Produced by Alberta Theatre Projects, 1979.

Pollock, Sharon. *The Wreck of the National Line Car*, Unpublished, Produced by Alberta Theatre Projects, 1978.

Reaney, James. *Apple Butter*, Talonbooks, Vancouver, 1978.

Reaney, James. *Geography Match*, Talonbooks, Vancouver, 1978.

Reaney, James. *Ignoramus*, Talonbooks, Vancouver, 1978.

Reaney, James. *Names and Nicknames*, Talonbooks, Vancouver, 1978.

Patterson, Pat, Dodi Robb, Joy Alexander and Pat McKelvey. *Jacob Two-Two Meets the Hooded Fang*, From the Book by Mordecai Richler, Unpublished, Produced by Young People's Theatre, 1979.

Robb, Dodi and Pat Patterson. *The Dandy Lion*, New Children's Drama 2, new press, Toronto, 1972.

Robb, Dodi and Pat Patterson. *Little Red Riding Hood*, New Children's Drama 2, new press, Toronto, 1972.

Robb, Dodi and Pat Patterson. *The Popcorn Man*, New Children's Drama 2, new press, Toronto, 1972.

Rosen, Sheldon. *Shadowdance*, Based on an Idea by Yurek Bogajewicz, Created in Participation with Pat Best, Stuart Nemtin, Menlo Skye MacFarland and David MacLean, Unpublished, Produced by Green Thumb Players, 1977.

Salutin, Rick and Theatre Passe Muraille. *1837: The Farmers' Revolt*, James Lorimer & Co., Toronto, 1976.

Salutin, Rick. *Money*, Unpublished, produced by Young People's Theatre, 1971.

Singer, Ron. *God is Alive and Well and Living in Heaven*, Unpublished, Produced by Young People's Theatre, 1971.

Smyth, Donna E. *Susanna Moodie,* Unpublished, Produced by Mermaid Theatre, 1976.

Truss, Jan. *The Judgement of Clifford Sifton,* Playwright's Co-op, Toronto, 1979.

Truss, Jan. *Oomeraghi Oh!,* Playwright's Co-op, Toronto, 1978.

Truss, Jan. *Thung-a-ling-ring,* Unpublished, Commissioned by Wagon Stage, City of Calgary Parks and Recreation Department, 1977.

Truss, Jan. *A Very Small Rebellion,* Playwright's Co-op, Toronto, 1978.

Way, Brian. *The Bell,* Baker's Plays, Boston, 1977.

Way Brian. *The Clown,* Baker's Plays, Boston, 1977.

Way, Brian. *The Decision,* Baker's Plays, Boston, 1977.

Way, Brian. *The Dog and the Stone,* Baker's Plays, Boston, 1977.

Way, Brian. *The Mirror Man,* Baker's Plays, Boston, 1977.

Way, Brian. *On Trial,* Baker's Plays, Boston, 1977.

Wylie, Betty Jane. *Kingsayer,* Playwright's Co-op, Toronto, 1978.

Wylie, Betty Jane. *The Old Woman and the Pedlar,* Play-wrights' Co-op, Toronto, 1978.

Youtheatre. *Historyherstory,* Unpublished, Produced by Youtheatre, Montreal.

Zapf, Carolin. *The Players and the King's Servant,* Unpublished, Produced by Young People's Theatre, 1976.

Zapf, Carolin, *Simre the Dwarf,* Unpublished, Produced by Young People's Theatre, 1976.

Zipes, Jack. *Man oh Man, Political Plays for Children,* Telos Press, St. Louis, 1976.

Plays for Young Audiences in French Canada

Unless otherwise stated, the following texts have not been published:

Allaire, Serge. *Expédition J.O. (objectif Jupiter)*.

Barbeau, Jean. *Le Théâtre de la maintenance*.

Bebelle (la). *L'amour, c'est des toasts*, Collective Creation.

Bouchard, Diane. *L'Enfant de l'étoile*, Adapted from a Tale by Oscar Wilde.

Bouchard, Diane. *Il était une fois en Neuve-France*.

Cailloux, André. *François et l'Oiseau du Brésil*, Followed by *Tombé des étoiles*, Leméac, Montréal, 1977.

Cailloux, André. *Frizelis et la Fée Doduche*, Leméac, Montréal, 1973.

Cailloux, André. *Frezelis et Gros Guillaume*, Leméac, Montréal, 1973.

Cailloux, André. *L'Ile-au-Sorcier*, Leméac, Montréal, 1974.

Confettis (les). *La Bicyclette*, Collective Creation.

de Bellefeuille, Normand and André Lamarre. *Salomon*.

Depatie, François. *Le Cadran et le cerf-volant*.

Depatie, François. *En écoutant le coeur des pommes*.

Depatie, François. *Le Grand Jour*, Centre d'essai des auteurs dramatiques.

Depatie, François. *Luclac dans l'Infini*.

Garneau, Michel. *Sers-toi de tes antennes*, Centre d'essai des auteurs dramatiques.

Garneau, Michel, *et al. Pourquoi tu dis ça?*

Gauthier, Gilles. *On n'est pas des enfants d'école*.

Gingras, Luc. *Une journée au marché: le Moussem*.

Gurik, Renée and Robert Gurik. *Op-production*.

Hébert, Marie-Francine, *C'est tellement cute, des enfants*, Quinze, Montréal, 1975.

Hébert, Marie-Francine. *C't'assez plate*, Centre d'essai des auteurs dramatiques.

Hébert, Marie-Francine. *Une ligne blanche au jambon*, Leméac, Montréal, 1974.

Hébert, Marie-Francine. *Le Tour du chapeau*, Centre d'essai des auteurs dramatiques.

Hébert, Marie-Francine. *Tu viendras pas patiner dans ma cour*, Centre d'essai des auteurs dramatiques.

Lacannerie and Denis Lagueux. *Catherine est pas contente,* Centre d'essai des auteurs dramatiques.

Lacannerie and Denis Lagueux. *Celui qui le dit, c'est lui qui l'est,* Centre d'essai des auteurs dramatiques.

Lacannerie and Denis Lagueux. *Chez-nous, c'est chez-nous,* Centre d'essai des auteurs dramatiques.

Lacannerie and Denis Lagueux. *On s'est encore écarté,* Centre d'essai des auteurs dramatiques.

Lahaye, Louise. *Chus pas ben dans mes culottes.*

Lahaye, Louise, *Impromptu chez Monsieur Pantalon.*

Laroche, Roland and Gilles Marsolais. *Opération-Théâtre.*

Leclerc, Félix, *Le Fou de l'île,* Adapted by Denis Chouinard.

Lücker, Reiner and Ludwig Volker. *Faut pas s'laisser faire,* Adapted by Odette Gagnon, Centre d'essai des auteurs dramatiques.

Mainville, Patrick. *Faby en Afrique.*

Marmaille (la). *L'Age de Pierre,* Collective Creation.

Morency, Pierre. *Marlot dans les merveilles,* Leméac, Montréal, 1975.

Morency, Pierre. *Tournebire et le Malin Frigo,* Leméac, Montréal, 1978.

Pomrenski, Micheline. *L'Abeille entre la ruche et la fleur.*

Pomrenski, Micheline. *La Forêt merveilleuse.*

Rhéault, Nicole-Marie. *Qui est le roi?*

Saint-Laurent, Andrée. *L'Enfant-Robot.*

Tessier, Evelyne. *A L'ombre du cactus.*

Théâtre de Carton (le). *Au coeur de la rumeur,* Collective Creation.

Théâtre de Carton (le). *Te sens-tu serré fort,* Collective Creation.

Théâtre de l'Oeil (le). *Tohu-Bohu.*

Théâtre de l'Oeil (le). *Le Toutatous.*

Théâtre des Pissenlits. *Les Ballons enchantés*

Théâtre des Pissenlits. *Tit-Jean, Margoten et le mauvais génie.*

Yendt, Maurice. *Histoire aux cheveux rouges,* Les Cahiers du soleil debout, Lyon, France.

Index

We wish to thank the following for various unwritten exchanges about children and theatre in Canada. Their ideas have been invaluable in supplementing our attendance at plays and our studies of company records: Richard Courtney, Rex Deverell, Quenten Doolittle, Ruth Frost, Evelyn Garbary, Keith Johnstone, Judith Koltai, Ken Kramer, Sue Kramer, David Lander, David Latham, Jonathan Levy, Herb Lewis, Lee Lewis, Tom Miller, Douglas Riske, Susan Rubes, Gloria Shapiro, Donald Truss, Jan Truss, Lucille Wagner and Betty Jane Wylie.

We wish to acknowledge Barbara Parish for her assistance with the manuscript.